GEORGE
PIDGEON

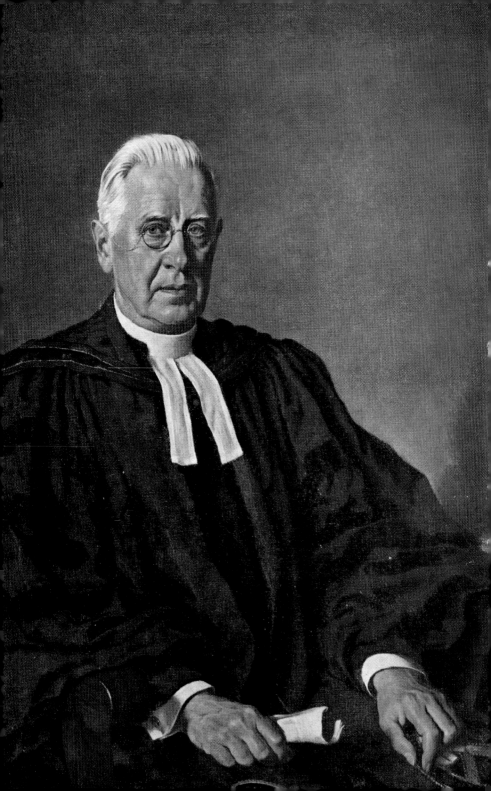

GEORGE PIDGEON

A Biography by
JOHN WEBSTER GRANT

Foreword by
THE HON. DONALD M. FLEMING
With a Portrait by
KENNETH FORBES

Toronto, The Ryerson Press

Published 1962

PRINTED AND BOUND IN CANADA BY THE RYERSON PRESS, TORONTO

To the Very Reverend
GEORGE CAMPBELL PIDGEON
D.D., LL.D.

Foreword

by the Honourable Donald M. Fleming, P.C., Q.C., M.P., B.A., LL.B., D.C.L.

It is eminently fitting that in this year 1962, when Dr. Pidgeon has attained his ninetieth birthday, an authentic biography of this great Church leader should be published. It is equally fitting that the task and honour should have fallen to Dr. John Webster Grant, the distinguished editor of The Ryerson Press.

The contribution of leaders to the history of their times often cannot be accurately assessed until years after the close of their lives. This is no less true of ecclesiastical leaders. Dr. Pidgeon has, however, lived to such an advanced age and the fruits of his long labours have assumed such definite form that it is possible now to undertake such an assessment of his life's work. Judged by any standard his contribution to the history of his times has been enormous. Few persons in any walk of life have exerted so strong an influence in the shaping of events and the moulding of thought in the past half-century in Canada as has George Campbell Pidgeon.

It was in the year 1920 that, as a fifteen-year-old boy visiting in Toronto, I first worshipped in Bloor Street Church and heard Dr. Pidgeon preach. His subject was "The Still Small Voice." I shall never forget that experience. A year later, as a student at the University of Toronto, I became a member of "Bloor St." For a quarter of a century, until his retirement in 1948, Dr. Pidgeon was my minister. I lived under the spell of his preaching from week to week. I followed his message through the days of decision on church union, through the grim days of controversy, through his leadership of the new-born United Church of Canada, through the years of economic depression, through World War II, through the years of post-war growth, and through the years of his devoted service to the ecumenical movement in Canada and abroad. For thirty years I have been closely associated with him in the Business Men's Noonday Bible Club, and also the Session, the Sunday School and the Board of Missions. I count myself one of Dr. Pidgeon's spiritual sons.

This volume is all too brief. Nevertheless, Dr. Grant has achieved a comprehensive and balanced treatment of Dr. Pidgeon's life, his message and his service. The influence of his boyhood home and especially of his mother, to whom he referred so frequently and reverently throughout the years, his own happy married life sustained by the devotion of his wife and three children, the years of preparation for the tasks of leadership, have all found their recognized place in this biography. His rise to leadership in the church and his role in the history of the nation have here been faithfully chronicled. Not the easiest task of the biographer was to review and assess the events associated with church union. Inevitably the history of that movement and its culmination in 1925 play a large role in this biography. It could not have been otherwise. Dr. Pidgeon was the central figure in it. It remains his greatest achievement. The author has treated this period in Dr. Pidgeon's life with fairness, objectivity and restraint.

Dr. Grant has correctly stressed the role which the sheer quality of character has played in Dr. Pidgeon's career: "He was a centre of calm in a whirlwind of hysteria. . . . Of all the assets that George Pidgeon brought to the leadership of the unionist cause the greatest were qualities of character. Even in the bitterest days of controversy few suspected his motives or doubted his integrity. And even beyond integrity he showed forth a quality of sanctity that disarmed criticism. . . . George Pidgeon was a fighting saint of unity."

It was said of him when the currents of bitter controversy were swirling that he was the only man who kept his head. The Reverend R. E. Knowles writing at the time described him as "the saintly Pidgeon" and the "divinely stubborn Pidgeon."

With infinite kindness and charity in its most comprehensive sense Dr. Pidgeon has always combined gentleness, restraint, constancy and humility with firm determination. He has never shown any patience toward cant and hypocrisy. Having chosen his goal and his course in the light of conscience he would not be deterred by controversy or criticism, no matter how rancorous or bitter. No man has ever been possessed of a more absorbing sense of dedication to Jesus Christ.

Dr. Pidgeon's preaching ministry is without parallel in Canada. He delivered his first sermon at the age of sixteen in 1888, his most recent one in 1960 at the age of eighty-eight. That ministry of the Word spans seventy-two years—a record in itself. He was the consistently greatest preacher of his time in Canada. The pulpit he occupied demanded a very high standard of scholarship, intellectual excellence and literary erudition. He always spoke from the Bible. As one person expressed it, "His mind is simply saturated with the Scriptures"—a rare tribute in our times. His aim was to seek total commitment to Jesus Christ, to strengthen faith, to teach, to instruct, to uplift. How often he has dwelt on the theme of the spiritual rebirth, the growth in grace, the deepening of the Christian life and experience! No man ever presented more consistently the Christian evangel. To the end of his ministry he offered his hearers, particularly the students, in direct and uncompromising terms "my Christ." To what better source can we turn for the message he preached than his own words in the Foreword to his book *The Indwelling Christ:*

I have been trying in these closing months of my active ministry to give the essence of the Gospel I have preached through the years. Its centre has been the living Christ. What I have asked young Christians to confess as they became members of the Church in full communion I have tried to set forth in these expositions—the experience of Christ as Saviour and obedience to Him as Lord.

I suppose I have heard Dr. Pidgeon in the pulpit, in the Business Men's Noonday Bible Club and elsewhere deliver more than a thousand sermons and addresses. I do not believe he every essayed one of them unprepared. To have entered the pulpit without due preparation, mental and spiritual, would have been to him a blasphemy. The most sublime sermon I ever heard him deliver was one at the very height of the church union controversy on the text, "By this shall all men know that ye are my disciples, if ye have love one to another." It was at a communion service at Bloor Street Church. It was so moving that the elders, pro-union and anti-union, exchanged handshakes with one another during the service in full view of the congregation.

A year and a half later, on his return to his pulpit after months of travel as Moderator of The United Church of Canada visiting congregations in all parts of Canada, his sermon on the text "Mine own vineyard have I neglected" will always live in memory. The veneration in which his congregation held him bordered on idolatry.

There can be no great preaching very long without great praying. Dr. Pidgeon's prayers were always in themselves a benediction. They were a heart's complete outpouring. They were not read. He employed imagery with sublime effect. I recall one, "As the flowers turn their faces to the sun, so do we lift our faces and our hearts to Thee, our God and Creator."

No account of Dr. Pidgeon's ministry can be complete without reference to the lives he touched. Probably no preacher in Canada has ever influenced so many students who have gone forth to be leaders in all walks of life. His personal friendship has been the prized possession of many leaders in business, industry, finance, the professions and public life. His counsel and prayers were available to them always.

Dr. Grant has closed Chapter II of this volume with a paragraph which contains a most penetrating observation. It sums up admirably the secret of Dr. Pidgeon's ministry:

In the end the remarkable effectiveness of his ministry can be explained only by the depth and solidity of its spiritual foundations. . . . Few have been so rich in the wisdom that is acquired through constant prayer and meditation on the Scriptures. The habit of ordering his life through daily communion with God gave Pidgeon a poise and a presence that . . . enabled him to wait out crises in the assurance that the right answers would be given. As he moved among his people he made them aware of another dimension of being, and they responded by accepting his conviction that only the best can fitly be offered to God.

For George Campbell Pidgeon, the true servant of the living God, there is surely stored up a crown of glory that fadeth not away.

Ottawa, July 8, 1962

Preface

During the past few years, in a series of dictated memoranda,
Dr. Pidgeon has recalled some of the incidents of his life and
described some of the movements in which he has taken part.
When it was originally proposed that I should be associated
with him in the writing of his memoirs, I intended merely to
put these notes together in a connected narrative. I discovered, however, that although set down with admirable
clarity, Dr. Pidgeon's reminiscences do not by any means tell
the whole story of his life. I also learned that the Archives
of The United Church of Canada have an excellent collection
of letters and papers dealing with Dr. Pidgeon's contribution
to the union of churches in 1925, and that Dr. Pidgeon has in
his own possession a complete set of office files covering the
period of his ministry at Bloor Street Church. This book owes
a great deal to Dr. Pidgeon's reminiscences, but as finally
written it is my work and I take complete responsibility for
all the judgments expressed in it.

When using unpublished material, I have tried to relieve
the reader as much as possible of burdensome documentation
without obscuring the sources of my information. Where I
have referred to letters or other documents, it may be assumed
that they are from files either in the Archives or in Dr.
Pidgeon's home. Information not credited to any source has
been obtained from Dr. Pidgeon himself through the typed
notes or by personal interview. Roughly speaking, the first

six Chapters depend almost entirely on Dr. Pidgeon's recollections; Chapters 7 to 9 are based largely on material in the Archives; Chapters 10 to 12 are from the personal files.

I should especially like to thank Mrs. W. E. M. Aitken, who typed notes from her father's dictation, made much of the material available to me at the cost of considerable inconvenience to herself, and gave me the benefit of her own recollections. I should like to thank Dr. Arthur G. Reynolds, who not only gave me the run of the Archives but looked up some valuable information for me. I should like to thank my secretary, Mrs. Betty Henley, who typed the manuscript. I should like to thank several friends and former associates of Dr. Pidgeon for passing on information and impressions, and for reading the manuscript.

Most of all I should like to thank Dr. Pidgeon for his generosity in making time available, for his readiness to answer questions, and for the keenness of his judgments. He has listened patiently to the retelling of his life story, making an occasional correction or injecting a gentle but shrewd comment, but not once attempting to put his actions in a better light. It has been a pleasure to work with him.

JOHN WEBSTER GRANT

June 20, 1962

Contents

GEORGE
PIDGEON

1. Grand Cascapedia

By 1831 most of the desirable river properties of the Maritime Provinces were occupied. When a lowland Scots capitalist named William Cuthbert sought a site for a lumber mill and settlement, it was therefore natural that he should turn to Quebec's Gaspé peninsula. The southern slope of the peninsula offered several large rivers, and a good proportion of the sparse population consisted of Protestants, of Loyalist or Channel Island origin. Cuthbert located between the mouths of the Grand and Little Cascapedia rivers, where his site commanded two river basins covered by magnificent stands of birch and maple. To run his mill he brought out a number of fellow-lowlanders and founded the village of New Richmond.

In the late nineteenth century New Richmond was still Paul Bunyan country, ideal for developing men of brawn and natural cunning. There were moose in the woods, and sometimes bears in the barnyard. Game was important to the pioneer's diet, and hunters developed unusual talents of resourcefulness in obtaining it. Peter Campbell of Escuminac, an uncle of George Pidgeon, was one who devised his own method of enlarging the bore of his gun so that it would not scatter shot, thus anticipating the widely touted choke-bore rifle that was officially invented twenty years later. Sailor, blacksmith, hunter and farmer, Campbell was a typical member of the frontier aristocracy of strength and adaptability. Unfortunately for the honest inhabitants of New

Richmond, the salmon fishery of the Cascapedia was for many years the preserve of wealthy sportsmen and governors general, but game laws had a limited effect on the frontier.

The country that nourished the hunter was not so hospitable to the farmer. The backbone of the Gaspé peninsula is a range of mountains, the Shickshocks, and although the southern slope is the gentler, the farmer's first task was to clear thickly wooded hills. Archibald Pidgeon, a planner as well as a pioneer, made up his mind from the beginning which areas he would eventually bring into cultivation. Each summer he set himself and his boys a stint of clearing. Eventually he was clearing shorthanded, for his son George had gone off to college, but he had no thought of stopping short of his goal. At last he was able to say, "Now I have it cleared," and perhaps his work was a little easier after that. But the land can never have been the most fertile: today no one lives on the old farm, and the house has gone.

Although life in pioneer New Richmond was wholesome and usually enjoyable, it was by no means an uninterrupted idyll. A common struggle against nature encouraged hospitality and a brand of kindliness that was free from softness and sentimentality. The rough frontiersman was, however, apt to lack the habits of self-control that in a more settled society enable people to live together without too much obvious friction. His vices were those of intemperate self-expression—violence, drunkenness and profanity, or general indifference to property rights.

To the ills of a lumbering community, religion was a prime antidote. Unlike the better-known frontier of the Wild West, New Richmond never went through a period of ungodliness. The first minister arrived in 1833, and although he did not remain long, the Church of Scotland soon sent a replacement. The church was without question the social and ideological centre of New Richmond, as it was the centre of most Canadian villages of the nineteenth century. There were, indeed, no rivals. There were no movies, no radio or television, no community centre except the church porch. Government departments showed little interest in rural life except to collect modest taxes. Schoolteachers, who qualified by proving they had a tolerable writing hand, were usually in no position to challenge the intellectual supremacy of the minister. In most homes the Bible was the only book available. Christian belief was universal, and a high level of biblical literacy was maintained.

In a frontier settlement, religion played a clear and important moral role. This role was not primary, since it was a matter of first principle that "man's chief end is to glorify God and to enjoy him forever." The Christian life as a matter of course took into account the existence of another world more important and infinitely more lasting than this. In the circumstances, however, the truths of the gospel were most readily grasped as they impinged on the frailties of simple people.

In New Richmond the church had to contend not with doubt or disbelief or moral ambiguity, but with sin of the most obvious and carnal, although not ordinarily the most vicious, kind. Temptation was easy to recognize but not always easy to resist. The church accordingly provided strong and stable sanctions for the encouragement of honesty and respect for law, of continence and abstinence, and of kindness and neighbourliness. It also provided the strong and stable support of preaching, sacraments and discipline. The sanctions and the support were effective among those who took advantage of them, transmuting brawn into moral fibre. The immoral were in general those who neglected the practice of religion, and the efforts of the church were therefore directed more to admonishing the careless than to condemning the wicked.

The church was the isolated settlement's link with the outside world. New Richmond was in those days far from a railroad. George Pidgeon tells of one occasion when his brother Leslie took a sleigh across the ice of the Baie de Chaleur from the nearest station at Dalhousie, New Brunswick. It was late in the season, and the ice was already melting. There were signs of a fresh track, however, and Leslie decided that if another could make it, so could he. But the other outfit had started out only to turn back. The ice was in such poor condition that at every step water came up around the horse's feet. Leslie could only keep the horse going and hope for the best. He reached the other shore safely, but at the next tide the ice was carried right out of the bay. In summer even this hazardous short cut was impossible, and it was necessary to make a long drive and then take a ferry to Campbellton on the Intercolonial line.

The church could do little about physical isolation, but it furnished whatever mental stimulus there was. There were no daily newspapers, so denominational magazines, and such semi-religious periodicals as the Montreal *Witness*, provided news and views on public and church affairs. Through their interest in Christian missions abroad, they also imparted a knowledge of so-called heathen lands that has only recently become widely available elsewhere. Sermons too contributed to a widening of interest. Although the ministers of New Richmond were fairly conservative, they were educated men who shared with their people the latest trends of thought at university and theological college. George Pidgeon recalls that he was familiar with the names of such German theologians as Schleiermacher and Ritschl before he had ever left the Gaspé coast.

The Protestant inhabitants of New Richmond were almost without exception Presbyterians, heirs to the religious traditions of reformed Scotland. Presbyterianism took root with amazing speed in Maritime soil. Well planted before the home churches had established efficient missionary organization, the local church set up presbyteries and ordained ministers without much consultation with Scottish authorities. Soon it was recruiting and training its own ministers. Although still representing a tiny community, by 1846 the Synod of Nova Scotia had sent John Geddie of Prince Edward Island as its first missionary to the New Hebrides in the south seas. Anyone familiar with the struggles of larger Canadian churches to achieve independence from British subsidy and control will marvel at the vigour of these ministers and congregations, who became self-governing, self-supporting and self-propagating almost from the time they landed in the Maritimes. The result of such vigour was to engender a self-confidence that could either degenerate into smugness or inspire a remarkable sense of divine mission.

Maritime Presbyterianism was dogmatically Calvinistic, and as rigid in its application of a puritanical moral code as the critics of Calvinism complain. An old-time "sabbath" was, by modern standards, forbidding to the extreme. On Saturday wood was cut and food prepared, children bathed and men shaved. On Sunday there would be no unnecessary labour and, among the stricter ones, no house-to-house visits.

Methods of maintaining the tradition were simple but effective. Sermons and sabbath-school classes were biblical in theme, doctrinal and moral in application. Children were expected to commit to memory the Shorter Catechism of the Westminster Assembly, and in earlier days ministers tested their students' knowledge by "catechizing" them in their homes. The annual communion seasons were times of self-examination and mutual examination, as elders scrutinized the records of members of the congregation. To submit one's conduct and character to such an inquisition was no light responsibility: many devout Christians postponed "going forward" until they believed themselves beyond human reproach. The same impression of seriousness was implicit in the austere solemnity of the worship itself, simple but vested with the authority of high pulpit and sparkling white sacramental linen.

Despite its refusal to compromise with the flesh, Presbyterianism as practised in New Richmond was a popular faith, maintained by kindly men and women who delighted in it. Those who condemn the old Calvinism as a tyranny of minister and Kirk session are apt to forget that the system could not have endured apart from its foundation of family worship and individual Bible reading. The true high priest of Presbyterian worship was the head of the family. It was Archibald Pidgeon himself who each day made sure that his sons did their reading, who at the end of the day called for the Book, and who on sunny sabbaths determined that the hay that had been rained on through the week should still remain ungathered. He was not so superstitious as to expect material reward for his obedience to divine decrees. "He lost his hay," an observer commented, "but he saved his sons."

Presbyterianism was popular too in its encouragement of theological discussion. Although its usual approach to the Bible was what we should today call fundamentalist, differences in biblical interpretation were actively encouraged. Theological debate reached its ritual climax on the Friday before communion, when on the day of the *ceisd,* or questioning, it was the responsibility of one elder to propound a theological question for discussion by other elders. The presiding minister spoke last, risking severe loss of face if he failed to improve on earlier statements. This same spirited discussion was normal in the Bible class and in the family post-mortem on the sabbath sermon. Presbyterians seldom spoke of their religion when they were with strangers, but within the family circle there was no such reticence. These discussions might lead to few radical conclusions, but they left no room for obscurantism.

The hostility to book learning so conspicuous in some frontier areas was alien to the spirit of Presbyterian New Richmond. The Scottish reformers of the sixteenth century, associating Roman Catholicism with the backward state in which they found their country, had regarded education as the natural handmaid of Protestantism. Thomas McCulloch, eager that early-nineteenth-century Nova Scotia should provide for her own ministry, had transmitted this enthusiasm for education to his struggling fellow-pioneers. The minister of the village was often its most effective schoolmaster.

The religion of New Richmond had warmth, despite Calvinism's reputation for dourness. Scots were suspicious of introspective personal testimonies and of displays of emotion, but their evangelical groups had left a heritage of religious conviction that was private but deeply felt. When in the 1880's a Baptist evangelist named Vincent set a revival in motion on the Gaspé frontier, Mr. Lindsay, the Presbyterian minister, soon assumed its leadership. When he discouraged sensationalism, some parishioners left his church in disgust and turned to the Plymouth Brethren. But most found it possible to combine Presbyterianism with revivalism, and the spiritual pulse of the community was quickened.

Although remote from urban centres, New Richmond was affected by the changes of outlook that industrialization was introducing. Church and community life were apparently unchanged, but rigid Calvinism was no longer unquestioned and the critical re-examination of the Bible was becoming known. Already in the 1860's Methodist itinerants started a vigorous debate on the question of free will. The revival furthered the change, for it challenged the old identification of religion with accepted patterns of belief and conduct. A student named J. F. Smith was one so affected. Attending a revival meeting in Halifax with the intention of breaking it up, he was so impressed that he returned to his native coast with an openness of mind that led him to accept more new ideas than the evangelists had given him. New Richmond remained sound, but it was no longer static.

The most significant products of Presbyterianism in eastern Canada were men and women who were careful and opinionated but kindly and resourceful. A boy growing up in New Richmond would have every encouragement to gratify his desire for knowledge, and the greater his curiosity about the world, the more likely he would be to seek support and guidance from the church.

When William Cuthbert died on a visit to Scotland about the year 1847, his property was divided equally between his wife and his daughter Alice Thornton. Neither could run the mill, but fortunately Mrs. Cuthbert had a brother who had already been brought into the business. Robert Montgomery took his son, Robert Hudson Montgomery, into partnership, and the family retained control until well into this century.

The Montgomery family had long been established in Prince Edward Island—one descendant was the author of *Anne of Green Gables*. Like other settlers, they were prevented by a system of absentee tenure from securing a clear title to their lands. When they took over the Cuthbert mill, therefore, the Montgomerys invited Mary Pidgeon, the widowed sister of Robert and of Mrs. Cuthbert, to bring her family over. Several of Mary Pidgeon's children were

grown sons who were anxious to farm, so on May 4, 1849, the
family moved to New Richmond.

This was not the first connection between the Pidgeon
family and the Gaspé peninsula. In 1798 the Reverend
Edward Pidgeon had been sent to the New Carlisle area by
the Antiburgher Synod of Scotland. He was the first Protestant
minister known to have worked on the coast. Of Huguenot
descent, he had been born in Yarmouth, England, and given
his theological training in Scotland. He soon left the Gaspé
peninsula and returned to Britain, only to come out again
under the auspices of the London Missionary Society.* In
1805 he moved to Prince Edward Island, where he married
Mary Montgomery and founded his family. In 1811 he was
called to the congregation of St. Peter's Bay. Ill health forced
his retirement in 1820. He died in 1843 while attending
service in what is now the Geddie Memorial Church at New
London.

The appearance of John Geddie's name in the Pidgeon story
is more than fortuitous. Geddie had conducted a Bible class
for young men while still a pastor at New London. He taught
his pupils so thoroughly that they were somewhat frightened
of him, but the results of his teaching were to remain. Several
of the Pidgeon boys were in the class, and they took their
training with them to New Richmond.

In those days marriage was almost unthinkable for a farmer
without land. That may explain why the Pidgeon sons all
went to New Richmond as single men, although the eldest was
thirty-nine. The family first took land on a point at the
mouth of the Grand Cascapedia River. Later most of the
boys bought sections of the Cuthbert holdings further up the
river, although Hugh settled in the village of New Richmond.

---

*This is the family tradition. William Gregg states that he had come
out originally under the auspices of the London Missionary Society.
History of Presbyterianism in the Dominion of Canada (Toronto,
Presbyterian Printing and Publishing Co., 1885), p. 115.

Archibald, the youngest son, was seventeen at the time of the move. Still unmarried after Confederation when the Intercolonial Railway was being built, he secured a construction job near Campbellton, New Brunswick. Now and then he returned home on a visit; the distance was too great for a single day's travel, so he was grateful for the hospitality of John Campbell, who kept open house for travellers at Aboyne in the Escuminac district of Quebec. Archibald Pidgeon married Mary Campbell in 1871.

John Campbell, a stone-mason, had brought his wife, Elspeth Sutherland, to Aboyne about 1830. Of Roman Catholic background, he and his wife belonged to the established Kirk but later joined the Free Church. Like the Pidgeons, the Campbells were devout Christians and well-instructed Presbyterians.

Archibald Pidgeon took his bride to a farm not far from the mouth of the Grand Cascapedia River. The house was on top of a hill, and in typically Scottish fashion it was located almost a mile from the road. Archibald had bought the farm from his cousin Mrs. Thornton, and he was still paying for it when he married. Mrs. Thornton then asked him to take over another farm four miles up the river. He did so, and for many years took hay off the intervale, but thieving settlers prevented him from claiming much of the lumber. He cannot have pressed his rights very hard. Later, when his son Hugh John had taken over and brought one of the trespassers to boot, the comment was, "He's not nearly as fine a man as his father."

George Campbell Pidgeon was born on March 2, 1872, the eldest son of Archibald and Mary Pidgeon. Leslie followed in 1873, Elsie in 1874, and Hugh John in 1876.

In a pious community Archibald and Mary Pidgeon were people of exceptional piety. It is only natural, perhaps, that

George Pidgeon should recall his parents as people altogether out of the ordinary, for most children think of their parents in these terms. Most significant in the son's recollection, perhaps, was his conviction that what gave his boyhood home its special character was the combination of two different but complementary influences. Dr. Pidgeon best describes his parents in his own words:

Mother was the most intensely religious person I have ever known. God was in all her thoughts. Her prayer life, her knowledge of the Bible, her vigorous thinking and strong convictions we felt every hour. Her claim for us was for a higher moral level than that of the community around us, and for a thoughtfulness that took in all the experiences of life. We always felt that it would have killed her if any of us had fallen into the vices of so many around us in that primitive community. She was a Calvinist in her theology, a theology based on the New Testament. But it was our birth into the life of Christ that was the passion of her soul.

Father was possessed with his father's love of learning. As a young farmer he would provide for the care of his stock in winter while he went to school. The learning which he thirsted for, but had never been able to get, he claimed for his children, and especially for me. The only time I ever heard him come into the house irritated and complaining was one evening after he had failed to get the little school reopened for us. . . .

Father read the Bible thoughtfully. He faced the problems honestly, never shirking its difficulties.' One day Leslie came in and found him and Uncle Peter Campbell with their heads together, deeply wrapped in a Bible problem. They were discussing the fate of Jephthah's daughter.

What a boon modern learning would have been to them!

Dr. Pidgeon adds that despite the lack of "modern learning" the father had renounced the older Calvinism, finding its harsh predestination incompatible with the neighbourliness of New Richmond life. The mother was apparently a simpler and more conservative person, but her exceptional moral stamina left an indelible mark upon her children.

As the family of four grew up on the Cascapedia farm, the church with its high pulpit played an increasingly important part in their lives. Although the farm chores had to be done on Sundays as on other days—despite Calvin!—the parents always succeeded in taking at least one of their children for the five-mile drive and slow ferry run that took them to eleven o'clock service. In the afternoon there would be a brief visit. Then, after an hour spent with the father learning by heart a question in the Shorter Catechism, the pair would end the day with a quiet walk through the fields under the westering sun. Dr. Pidgeon recalls his Presbyterian sabbaths at home with obvious pleasure.

The children were reaching adolescence when the religious revival was at its height, and George especially was affected for life by its evangelical emphasis. Indeed, George Pidgeon must have been a boy of exceptional religious sensibilities. He has written an account of the decisive season when he went forward as a communicant in the church, an event that took place while he was staying with his Uncle Hugh and Aunt Lorina in order to attend the Black Cape school:

They left me to myself that Saturday evening as, in the light of the lamp, I read again the account of that first communion service in preparation for my own first communion. As I read the story of Jesus' sacrifice I seemed to be going with him step by step through the trial and the mockery and the suffering of death for me. Then the service the next day. But even that service led by our minister whom I revered seemed to take a second place beside that Saturday evening's communion as I prepared to join the congregation the next morning. Surely He was with me then sealing me for the communion and the services of the years that followed.

Despite an unusual intensity of religious feeling, George Pidgeon must have grown up with his brothers and sister as a boy of normal impulses. He recalls that he and Leslie were impetuous and eager, always embarking on new and sometimes impractical adventures. Elsie provided the balance, although younger than either, having a sense of reality that sprang from strong conviction rather than from lack of imagination. Hugh John was, of all of the children, the one who most readily understood the father. It was he who eventually took over the farm, and when ill health compelled him to leave it, the father was heartbroken.

Even in childhood, the pattern of the future was beginning to emerge. The four used to play a game that was probably common enough then, although now out of fashion, that of re-enacting the Sunday service. George was always the preacher; his pulpit, the family wood-pile behind the house.

2. The Making of a Preacher

By the 1880's the rural areas of eastern Canada supported more people than they do today, but even then they had passed their peak of self-contained abundance. There was still the prospect of a good living for the son who stayed on the family farm, but families were large and the others had little choice but to leave. Those with an aptitude for the land could hope to establish themselves in the west, then beginning to open up. Others made for the cities, still more often than not those of the northern United States. Whatever the destination, most young men migrated from the countryside. The era was one that distinguished sharply between success and failure. Especially in regions remote from cities, the recognized key to success was education. There was a general scramble to get to university, and through university into one of the professions. The Christian ministry was the goal of many. The prevalence of religious conviction made it both an honourable and a consecrated calling, and it had the advantage of requiring a comparatively small outlay of capital. Few pious lads could have failed to consider it as a possible life work, and most parents were delighted to entrust their sons to it.

Those who aspired to university had to clear two hurdles, especially formidable if they came from a relatively un-developed area like the Gaspé coast. One of these was the poor quality of country schools, which were meagrely equipped and staffed by teachers with little more education than their pupils. Only students with considerable ability to fend for themselves could hope to acquire an academic background that would carry them through matriculation, and even they were immeasurably helped if they were lucky enough to draw one or two teachers who knew how to discover and encourage a latent desire for learning.

The other hurdle was the almost universal lack of cash in farm homes. Farmers of the period could provide the "necessaries" on a scale that seemed opulent in comparison with pioneer days. Since their prosperity was based on a simple barter economy, however, few of them could begin to raise the sum required for higher education. Schoolteaching was a favourite device for earning one's way through college; but the method was painfully slow, often requiring as many years out of university as in. Fortunately the family solidarity of the period frequently came into play, and several members would pool their resources to educate one. All too often the process involved a family decision as to which son should be favoured, and many who faithfully kept their commitments hid feelings of bitter disappointment.

An impressive number of farm boys of the time succeeded in overcoming obstacles in Horatio Alger style; in the next generation they dominated the church and the universities, although they were not so conspicuous in politics and business. One could not say that they constituted a type, for they were stubbornly and sometimes eccentrically individual, but they had a number of common qualities. Their awareness of the almost miraculous nature of their rise from obscurity gave them a sense of personal destiny, a sense that was apt to be particularly strong when the family had selected and supported the member chosen to make his mark in the world. The difficulties of the way up further impressed upon them the importance of achievement, notably academic achievement. George Pidgeon tells of a student who gave keen competition in his theological classes at Montreal. Pidgeon led the second year and was slightly ahead during the third, when suddenly in class the competitor suffered a breakdown that was blamed for his death several years later. It would not have occurred to contemporaries to suggest that such strenuous effort might have been unwise.

The result was a generation that combined social responsibility and ambition without the least suspicion that the two might prove to be incompatible. A few years ago a common-room discussion among theological students led to the almost unanimous conclusion that the motive of Christian service was unlikely to lead one to a large city church. Men of Pidgeon's generation would not have followed the argument with much sympathy. They were on fire with the desire to give consecrated service, and they witnessed to their desire by giving an unprecedented number of recruits to overseas missions. But they had a concept of making good even in service that led them to value positions of unusual influence. They were not apologetic for ambition, although they would have been ashamed of laziness or inefficiency. They had the virtues—and the weaknesses—of David Riesman's "inner-directed" people. They were self-confident, self-reliant and adaptable, although sometimes lacking in the social graces and the ability to compromise. They would have described their personal ideal in terms of "character."

George Pidgeon was less than five years old when he first attended the little school at the Cascapedia River. He tells of the diffidence with which he began his education. The first day he got as far as his Uncle Dan's barn; on the second he reached the top of a high hill beyond his uncle's place; by the third he had reached the schoolhouse. There the methods must have been crude and often improvised. Slates were still standard equipment, and a teacher named Nat MacKenzie found it useful to offer lead pencils as rewards for special achievement. George received one for reciting the poem "Marco Bozaris."

Although most of the teaching at the one-room school was undistinguished, the Pidgeon children were fortunate in having one teacher whose influence became a lasting memory. Alice Nichols was an English girl whose academic qualifications were slight; she had barely secured her certificate. What she lacked in formal training, however, she made up in her love for the English language. She was the daughter of an old-fashioned English schoolmaster and had inherited from him a tradition of careful speech and writing. Throughout the vacations she maintained with the Pidgeon boys a correspondence in which she would carefully note errors and examples of poor usage in their letters. The most lasting of Alice Nichols' contributions was the successful transmission of her passion for craftsmanship in writing and speaking. And yet she was not fussy or sobersided. Dr. Pidgeon recalls that in search of excitement she would sometimes make three trips to New Richmond in a single day!

In time the children graduated to the larger school at New Richmond, known as a "model school" but superior in little but size. A year attending school at Black Cape was in many ways a welcome relief. Then closeness demanded a return to New Richmond, where a teacher named Robert Campbell made a formidable impression before some unrecalled difficulty caused him to leave in mid-term. Meanwhile George was being given instruction in Latin by the Reverend Peter Lindsay, remembered for a distinct hesitation in his speech but also for his enthusiastic sponsorship of the boys' education.

In the summer of 1887, J. H. F. Blue came to give special

classes to make up for the lost time. He had been at the school only a short time when he came down to the desk where George Pidgeon was sitting with his friend Ernest Gilker and said, "You boys can be ready for college this fall." The idea cannot have been a new one, at least to George. As long as he could remember he had planned to be a minister, and among Presbyterians there was no way into the ministry except through university and theological college. His parents and minister knew of his aim and supported it enthusiastically; indeed, his classes in Latin had no other purpose. But it is one thing to have a distant aim in view, and another to be confronted with the immediate possibility of its realization. George was only fifteen, and he had no doubt pondered the financial problem without finding a ready solution. He recalls that he was so startled by the proposal that he dared not mention it to anyone for some time.

The teacher had laid his plans thoroughly. He had obtained the agreement of the parents, although he could not persuade the Lindsays, and he had made a contact that led to the securing of the necessary financial help. Mrs. R. H. Montgomery, wife of the local mill-owner, and thus a cousin by marriage, was the natural leader and patron of all good works in the countryside. Approving Blue's plan, she sent for George. She told him she wanted to pay for the first two years of his college course and urged that false pride should not be allowed to interfere with her desire to help. "I was speechless," Dr. Pidgeon writes. "But I went away with a purpose to co-operate, and when I got home I found her offer there ahead of me."

In the fall of 1887, George Pidgeon enrolled at Morrin College, an affiliate of McGill in Quebec City. He and Ernest Gilker were accepted for admission on Blue's certification alone, but as the teacher had drilled them through the summer on Xenophon and other classical texts, they were among the best prepared of the year.

At Morrin the dominant influence was that of George Weir, who had come from Queen's to teach classics. Weir was a perfectionist who drilled his classes in paradigms and would almost leap over his desk in anger when a mistake was made. He was also a warm-hearted teacher who succeeded in conveying to students his own enthusiasm for his subject. Thus Pidgeon acquired the foundation for a course in the liberal arts, passing the intermediate examination at the end of his second year.

Apart from a single inspiring teacher, Morrin had little to offer. Endowed in 1861 by a prominent merchant who belonged to the Kirk of Scotland, it became redundant after the union of 1875 and languished for lack of support. By the turn of the century the church appointed a committee to learn what had happened to the college, but the commissioners reported difficulty in finding anyone who would admit responsibility for it. Even in 1887 the college was in decline, the student body consisting of about a dozen undergraduates in arts. The principal, Dr. John Cook, was a man of keen intellect who had been the first moderator of the Presbyterian Church in Canada and at one time temporary head of Queen's University. But his staff was on the whole elderly and made little impression. The building itself, a jail converted to sacred use, could have done very little to brighten the atmosphere.

In 1889, Mrs. Montgomery's offer to finance two years at university expired. She not only continued her assistance, however, but later lent money to start Leslie on his career. Meanwhile Dr. Hastwell Thornton, a distant cousin and an ardent graduate of McGill, had convinced Mrs. Montgomery that George should transfer to McGill, offering to pay for any increase in cost the move might involve. Principal

MacVicar offered room and board in the residence of the Presbyterian College in Montreal, so there was no occasion to take advantage of his offer. In the fall, therefore, George registered in third year arts.

McGill was a much livelier environment for a bright student than Morrin, and Montreal was the scene of more significant action than Quebec. Academically, Honour English under Professor Charles E. Moyse seemed to offer the best prospects. George acquired from him a lifelong interest in early English poetry, and his sermon illustrations in later years reflected more than a casual acquaintance with *The Canterbury Tales* and *The Faerie Queene*. Dr. Pidgeon recalls no single teacher at McGill who impressed him as much as did George Weir of Morrin.

Declining an affiliated course that would have saved a year's study, George Pidgeon graduated from McGill in the spring of 1891. In the fall of the same year he entered the Presbyterian College at Montreal. To a young man whose interests were basically religious, the college offered more excitement than the university. Principal D. H. MacVicar, theologically a Calvinist of the old school, was intensely interested in public affairs; and at that time there were plenty of issues to keep controversy alive. The one that roused the deepest feelings was the agitation over the Jesuit Estates Bill, by which the Quebec legislature proposed to return to the Jesuits the proceeds of property that had been sold at the time of the suppression of the order. When the Dominion government gave its assent to the bill, the theological professors blazed with anger.

Presbyterians had been acutely involved in controversy in Quebec for some time. Charles Chiniquy, the Canadian pastor of a largely Canadian congregation at Kankakee, Illinois, had left the Roman Catholic Church in 1862 with some of his flock and had later joined the Canada Presbyterian Church. In 1876 he had come to Montreal, where he sought under Presbyterian auspices to win French Canada for Protestantism. Despite high hopes no mass movement took place, but MacVicar continued to be an active supporter of the Board of French Evangelization and an alert watchman for any denial of Protestant liberties. Under his regime, life at the Presbyterian College was a series of alarms, and students inevitably imbued something of the psychology of battle.

During George Pidgeon's student years controversy invaded the college itself.* John Campbell, professor of Old Testament at Montreal, delivered a lecture to the students of Queen's on February 26, 1893. His topic was "The Perfect Father or the Perfect Book?" and in the course of his remarks he suggested that scriptural passages presenting God as vengeful or unloving were imperfectly inspired. His line of approach was that of "gradual revelation," already familiar in academic circles but frightening to many Canadian Presbyterians. The lecture was reviewed unfavourably in the *Presbyterian Review*, and there was considerable public clamour. Montreal Presbytery began an investigation leading to the formal opening on September 12 of the last great heresy trial within Canadian Presbyterianism. The most unusual feature of the Campbell case was that two of the most prominent accusers were his own principal and Professor John Scrimger, his colleague in the teaching of the Old and New Testaments. The result of the trial was a conviction, due in part perhaps to Campbell's advocacy of certain views about the devil that even his best friends found difficult to defend, but the Synod

---

*For an account see J. T. McNeill, *The Presbyterian Church in Canada*, 1875-1925 (Toronto, General Board of the Presbyterian Church in Canada, 1925), pp. 207-209.

of Montreal and Ottawa, which was a higher body than the presbytery, closed the case in 1894 by agreeing to let Campbell sign a statement that convinced the court of his general orthodoxy. The decision was generally regarded as a victory for Campbell, and theological professors have since been allowed all the theological freedom they seem to require. In that final year of Pidgeon's course, the common room and the residence buzzed with heated discussions, and the students showed their sympathy for the suspended Campbell by visiting him in exile at home.

Student recollections of theological lectures are less exciting than the records of controversy would suggest. Principal MacVicar, appropriately enough, lined out the Calvinistic system with deliberation so that students could enter it in their notebooks, and he expected to read his words unaltered on examination papers. Scrimger, who was to become principal of the college in 1909, applied the Socratic method to the interpretation of the New Testament. Campbell, the heretic, delivered dry-as-dust lectures written twenty years earlier. Dr. Pidgeon recalls, however, that when Campbell had occasion to discuss the love of God he showed "the power of a blazing aside."

When George Pidgeon was in his final year of theology, Leslie was beginning arts at McGill. The father, who had dedicated George to the ministry from birth, had originally marked Leslie as the one to stay home on the farm. Persistence in this choice would have been disastrous, and Leslie had eventually been persuaded to enter the ministry. George, still a student but earning some money by preaching, undertook his support for the first year in conjunction with their sister Elsie. In accordance with the established pattern of family solidarity, Leslie later helped his brother Hugh John to set up a sawmill at Beaver Dam, near the old home.

Then as now, summer work on a home mission field was a normal part of the career of an aspirant to the ministry. Such service was not compulsory. It offered an opportunity for gaining experience that was especially important in a church operating on the call system, and despite low rates of pay it was one of the few ways in which most students could hope to secure an uninterrupted education. The main drawback of the system was its complete lack of any provision for preparation or supervision. The student was totally dependent on his own resources. He could teach himself a good deal about the techniques of preaching and pastoral care, or he could form bad habits that might last him the rest of his life. Fortunately most fields contained self-appointed critics willing to advise inexperienced students.

George Pidgeon was appointed to his first mission field at the end of his second year at Morrin College. Dr. Campbell, a minister from Renfrew who had lectured at Morrin, persuaded him that a place could be found as a minister's assistant. On that basis he applied for a field, but instead of receiving an assistantship, he found himself at the age of seventeen appointed to one of the church's oldest home mission fields. Declining would have offended the authorities and left an important area unmanned, so off he went to Darling township in Lanark county, Ontario. As ammunition he had the Bible, the Shorter Catechism and a good knowledge of Latin grammar.

A student on a summer field today is likely to spend a large proportion of his time organizing programmes and camps for young people, and he might make a reputation for himself merely by successfully operating a church vacation school. In those days preaching was recognized as the centre of any ministry, and in an established field like Darling many of the people were skilled sermon-tasters. Darling mission contained families scattered over a large area, necessitating a tour of three preaching points each Sunday, and frequent nights away from home on a round of itinerant visiting. It had the advantage that a single sermon would satisfy each Sunday's requirements, but despite this relief, the prospect to a seventeen-year-old beginner must have been awesome.

Dr. Pidgeon recalls his various mission fields largely in terms of his progress as a preacher. At Darling he began by working out each sermon in detail and taking into the pulpit notes of the key words of every sentence. This method worked reasonably well, but the preacher felt unduly tied to his manuscript. Necessity soon brought about a change. On two occasions, meetings were arranged in private homes, and the speaker could not see the notes. He had a moment of near-panic but, after some practice, a new freedom. The summer ended with a sense of satisfaction, although Dr. Pidgeon still feels that the appointment was a cruel blunder.

The summers of 1890 and 1891 were spent on the field of Waterford and Markhamville, which spread over Kings and Albert counties in New Brunswick. Here there were five preaching points, mostly halls and schoolhouses, and except on Sundays the student was expected to cover the ground on foot. The Presbyterians were almost all Scots, and most of them were Orangemen. Biblical literacy was at a high peak, and critics were even more demanding of their preacher than at Darling.

There was not much leisure for sermon preparation, but Pidgeon saw to it that there was plenty of opportunity for preaching. Several of the preaching stations had held services only on alternate Sundays. The new student felt that he could make little impression on people who heard him less than once a week, so he arranged weekly services everywhere by calling meetings on Monday and Tuesday evenings. The preacher was driving himself, but by this time he was sure of his powers. From the beginning he discarded his notes, and although the first delivery of a sermon was sometimes difficult, there were always four more opportunities.

In the fall of 1891, George Pidgeon accepted an invitation from a fellow student, W. D. Reid, to take joint charge of the suburban mission of Victoria Church in Point St. Charles, Montreal. During the winter the two students conducted services alternately, and the barrel provided the necessary sermons. Through April, May and June, Reid took full charge. George took this opportunity to spend some time at his home in New Richmond, preaching occasionally at Port Daniel and other places along the Gaspé coast.

During the remaining summer months, Pidgeon had full charge of Victoria Church, responsible for two sermons and a midweek address each week. He now decided to follow the advice of Dr. James Ross, who had just been appointed professor of practical theology, that he should write out the morning sermon in full but only jot down notes for the evening service. The experiment succeeded and became regular practice. Dr. Pidgeon insists, however, that he has never preached extemporaneously. He found that preaching from notes demanded even more thorough preparation than ever, for it was necessary at every point to know not only what he was going to say but how he was going to say it. During one summer he preached for three months without writing anything, but, he writes, this only meant that the whole preparation went on within his head.

I found myself forming sentences in my thinking and giving attention to expression and delivery as I had been doing with the pen. At the same time, this effort at mental composition did something for my public utterances that I could have attained in no other way.

Among the new members whom Reid enlisted at Victoria Church there was a Methodist named Stephen Jones. Jones was in charge of the furnace in the iron mill of Peck, Benny and Company; his wife, Mary Ball, was the daughter of an English Methodist minister who had come out to an iron mill at Troy, New York. Moving with their family of six to Point St. Charles, and finding no Methodist church there, they joined the Presbyterian cause and Stephen became an elder. George Pidgeon was soon a familiar visitor at the home, which reminded him very much of his own. He was especially attracted to Helen, the youngest member of the family and a graduate of Stanstead College. Further developments were to follow.

George Pidgeon's last student mission field was at Montreal Junction, later known as Montreal West. He began work there in the spring of 1893, remaining through the rest of his college course and after. In the spring of 1894, he graduated as gold medallist from the Presbyterian College. On May 29, he was ordained and inducted into the pastorate of Montreal West.

Graduation was not the end of formal study. Pidgeon immediately began work on a thesis that made him a Bachelor of Divinity in 1895. He then set out to obtain the rather rare Doctorate of Divinity in course from the Presbyterian College, taking as his field of study the Greek New Testament. He secured the degree in 1904, the youngest Canadian to have obtained the doctorate of divinity in this way. Throughout the intervening period he had related the topics of his prayer-meeting addresses to the subjects in which he would be examined.

3. Young Reformer

During the early years of George Pidgeon's ministry, industrialization was beginning to transform Canada from a pastoral
country into a land of cities and factories. When he was
ordained, the process was still so unobtrusive that most
Canadians were unaware of the revolution under way. The
encroachment of urban values was still mainly signalled by the
appearance of a few roadhouses on the outskirts of cities, by
a slight heightening of pressure upon the traditional British
Sunday, and by an increase in spending money that was apt to
find its way into saloons and brothels. There were still no
street cars on Sunday, however, and the Puritan conscience
had lost little of its vigour.

After 1900, the pace of change accelerated rapidly. Immigration encouraged industrial expansion, and Canadians has-
tened to display their new-found wealth. Newcomers brought
new mores, and natives began to question old rural standards.
Someone was heard to declare at a Cape Breton prayer meeting, "We are metropolitan in our aims, and we are becoming
metropolitan in our vices."*

Later it would become evident that change was beginning
to pose questions to which the churches had no immediate
answers, and that the church's position in Canadian society
was to be radically altered. For the moment, however, Christian leaders saw no reason for any loss of confidence. The

---

*Clarence Mackinnon, *Reminiscences* (Toronto, Ryerson, 1938), p.
140.

churches were at the zenith of their power and influence, and their moral authority was still seldom questioned. The present might be full of challenge, but there were few qualms about the future.

The self-confidence of Canadian Protestantism was not without reason, for within a century it had achieved a remarkable advance. Historians have observed that few settlers came to Canada for religious reasons, and a reading of the diaries of early missionaries will show that few of the settlers brought with them much religious zeal. By the end of the nineteenth century, however, the churches had succeeded in occupying the country. In the east, they had divided the rural countryside into manageable and usually self-supporting parochial units; in the west, they had been able to keep abreast of the first wave of immigration. In the cities imposing sanctuaries were rising, and in most cases congregations were filling them. The churches were recruiting their own ministers and building colleges to train them. They were consolidating themselves into national communions and developing the institutions they required to serve a nation. Some of their leaders were national figures.

In the face of change, the churches could point not only to their present success but to their proven ability to move with the times. Biblical criticism and theological innovation had caused much heart-searching and some controversy, but churchmen were accepting a new openmindedness with much less dissension than their colleagues in the United States. They were busy changing their methods, too, to bring them in line with the new demands of young people and of single men adrift in the new cities.

Nowhere was confidence higher than within the Presbyterian Church in Canada. Divided in earlier times by the memory of bitter disputes that were meaningless outside Scotland, Canadian Presbyterians had succeeded in cementing a union that was practically unanimous, and had forged ahead after it. Methodists, with their more centralized administration, were apt to take the lead in formulating national programmes; but Presbyterians had profited from dynamic leadership in the west, and had succeeded in sandpapering away the sharper edges of Calvinism without lapsing into theological chaos.

In later years, when some of the harsher aspects of industrialization had become clearly visible, many would demand in the name of the gospel sweeping changes in the economic order. Writers of the time agreed that in Canada the impact of large-scale European immigration was the major catalyst that precipitated radical Christianity. It is not surprising, however, that the first reaction of the churches was to see the new urbanism chiefly as a challenge to moral standards. Indeed, one can with some plausibility interpret the crusading zeal of the period not as a response to a new threat but as a dramatic effort to complete a process of moral reformation that had been going on since pioneering days. Having successfully occupied the promised land, the children of Israel were now girding themselves to drive out the remnants of the Canaanites.

During the late years of the nineteenth century and the early decades of the twentieth, the churches pressed a two-pronged attack upon unrighteousness. One thrust was directed towards those affected by temptation, the other against those who offered it.

The early years of urbanization in Canada were marked by an outburst of evangelistic activity. Its purpose naturally differed somewhat from that of evangelism as it is conceived today. Efforts to reach the unchurched were secondary, for comparatively few were unchurched. The primary purpose was to deal with the intellectual and moral problems of perplexed churchgoers, and by reaffirming Christian commitment to strengthen moral fibre. Crowds flocked to meetings, the wicked element was usually just enough in evidence to stimulate excitement, and campaigns were often highly successful. Although the long-term results are not very obvious today, the first effective Christian programmes for Canadian young people and students were worked out by graduates of these evangelistic crusades. What further results there might have been will never be known, for the First World War intervened.

The other prong of the attack was directed against those who made profits from unrighteousness. It is unlikely that the sins of the flesh were alarmingly on the increase, but it seems clear that for the first time in Canadian experience they were being exploited by commercial interests large enough to have a dominant influence on governments. The response was a determined effort to close out gambling houses, to clear red-light districts, and to make liquor difficult or impossible to obtain. This last effort came to be the central issue of the whole campaign. Movements for moderation or abstinence had been active throughout most of the nineteenth century, but the campaign for legislation speeded up in the seventies. The Women's Christian Temperance Union was founded in 1874, and thousands of young people were soon wearing the blue ribbons of the pledge. In 1878 the Canadian parliament passed the Scott Act, authorizing the provinces to institute local option. Agitation was at its peak during the nineties, when plebiscites in all provinces but Quebec showed majorities for prohibition, and although no effective action was taken at the time, the pressure was maintained for several decades.

The Methodists were natural leaders in the struggle for moral reform. Their societies had come into being in the course of a series of campaigns of mass evangelism, and the temperance movement was, in spirit, an evangelistic rally dedicated to a particular moral aim. The Methodist belief in the practicality of seeking individual perfection was also easily transferable to the realm of social action. Presbyterians were inhibited by their doctrine of election from putting too much faith in political or economic programmes. Nevertheless the difference was only one of degree. Canadian Presbyterianism had inherited from the Scottish sects a tradition of evangelical activism, and it had a strong wing dedicated to moral reform.

Among Presbyterians, two irreconcilable approaches to society were represented by two leading educators. Principal D. H. MacVicar of Montreal sought to apply to Canada the militant Scottish concept of a covenanted nation, recognizing Christianity as the warp of the social fabric and enforcing the moral principles of the decalogue. Principal George M. Grant of Queen's, who had received his boyhood training in the Kirk, saw the gospel as a leaven in a basically secular lump, and he opposed any attempt to turn the church into what might be construed to be a political machine or pressure group. Mac-Vicar's precept was, "Whenever you see something that needs to be done, do it." Grant, who was a public man as well as a churchman, feared that hasty action would intensify the emotional division of the Canadian people without achieving any lasting results. The two frequently clashed over the issues of evangelization among French-Canadians and prohibition. Mac-Vicar eagerly espoused both, whereas Grant deplored the sensational proselytism of Father Chiniquy and resisted attempts to identify the church with a particular solution of the problem of alcohol. Grant carried more weight in the country as a whole, but in a crisis MacVicar could carry a General Assembly.

Montreal West, where George Pidgeon served as a student
and later as an ordained minister, was in 1894 a new residential
suburb only five miles from the Windsor station. The congregation had held its first services in the CPR freight shed, but
the celebrated evangelist John McNeill had quickly secured
action on a church building with the appeal, "Just think of it!
Presbyterians worshipping in a shed!" Pidgeon soon exchanged
a single outside appointment at Mount Royal Vale for another
at Kensington on the road to Montreal. The pastoral work was
easy enough to suit a graduate student, but in a field so close
to Montreal moral issues were bound to arise.

Pidgeon took to his first congregation no preconceived plan
of social action, but both temperament and tradition inclined
him to the approach of MacVicar. He could have applied to
himself, as to MacVicar, words he used much later in a sermon
about St. Paul, "For him to believe anything was to take steps
to put it into effect; faith always drove him into action."[*]
Pidgeon respected MacVicar and Grant alike, but although
he never considered himself bound to MacVicar's theology,
he shared his interest not only in prohibition but in French-
Canadian evangelization, religion in the schools and improved
methods of Sunday School teaching. French evangelization
was a particular interest: he represented Quebec on the
national committee almost from the time of his ordination,
and he was to retain his membership even after he had moved
to Ontario.

An apparently unimportant incident very early in his ministry seems to have had a considerable influence on his later
actions. While at Victoria Church in Point St. Charles, his
colleague W. D. Reid had succeeded in having a notorious
grocer deprived of his liquor licence. As a result of this single

---

[*]*The Indwelling Christ* (Toronto, Clarke, Irwin, 1948), p. 63.

action, drunkenness apparently declined markedly in the community as a whole and poverty became less noticeable. Pidgeon concluded that opportunity is an important factor in intemperance, and that even making liquor harder to get is a partial cure for the problems it causes.

An opportunity to put these principles into practice was not long delayed. When the new preacher drove to his afternoon appointment at Mount Royal Vale, he had to pass a resort known as the "Half-way House," illegally open on Sunday and doing a roaring business. The roadhouse had a bad reputation in several ways, but it was so well protected by T. A. Trenholme, the Liberal councillor for Notre Dame de Grâce, that temperance people despaired of effective action. Pidgeon persisted, however, and a member of his congregation opposed Trenholme when the latter came up for re-election. The election was lost by a three-to-one margin, and a pledge by Trenholme that the resort would be closed on Sundays lapsed after a year. Three years later, however, the residents voted to close the "Half-way House." Pidgeon concluded that minority action against established evils is never ineffective, for the public must sooner or later act when its attention is called to them.

The pastorate of St. Andrew's Church, Streetsville, Ontario, to which George Pidgeon was inducted on March 29, 1898, was an interlude of relative calm. Twenty-one miles from Toronto, Streetsville was in the heart of the countryside in that era of buggies and dusty roads. The Presbyterian minister customarily drove one of the best horses in Peel county, and Pidgeon took pride in driving well. He needed a good horse to cover the large area of his congregation, but it was impossible to make the rounds quickly when each visit included a pressing invitation to a meal. Life in Streetsville at the turn of the century was free from distractions to an extent scarcely

conceivable today. Visiting concerts from Toronto and mis-
cellaneous entertainments by the local Bible class were high-
lights, and when the villagers wanted an account of the South
African war, they had to import a young veteran from Port
Credit.

Six days before his induction, George Pidgeon had married
Helen Jones, who brought to the Streetsville manse her music,
her wood-carving and her love of skating and snow-shoeing.
Soon the pair were being introduced by the various elders to
the families of their districts, were riding behind Queenie, or
were cycling together on rounds of pastoral visitation. Mrs.
Pidgeon always shared intimately her husband's pastoral work.
Forceful although unobtrusive, she invariably made the manse
a social centre for young people and won the confidence of the
women of the congregation. The people of Streetsville were
friendly, although the Pidgeons caused a mild scandal by taking a Roman Catholic maid into their house. The one intract-
able part of the environment was the manse itself; it had been
enlarged to thirteen rooms to accommodate a particularly
large clerical family, and Presbyterian polity required the minister to provide his own furniture. When Alice and Arch
arrived to begin the family, there was plenty of room for
them.

Pastoral work was satisfying but light, allowing the developing preacher ample time to prepare his sermons. His custom
was to spend the mornings from Monday until Wednesday in
his study, giving two hours to New Testament Greek and
exegesis, and then working on his sermon for two hours
more. On Thursday he normally spent the whole day on his
sermon, and then he reworked the material for oral delivery.
It was, he admits, a time-consuming method of preparation,
but at Streetsville time was available.

The great excitement of those years was the impact of the

Sunday School movement, then replacing Christian Endeavour as the current enthusiasm in the field of Christian education. Hitherto Sunday School instruction had depended almost entirely upon the initiative of the local minister. A programme for giving teachers systematic training, promoted in Canada by MacVicar and others, offered possibilities for effective work that had scarcely been glimpsed before. A curriculum was provided by the International Sunday School Lessons, which made joint training for teachers possible by setting identical lessons each Sunday for all grades.

The Sunday School movement caught the imagination of church people during the nineties, and Peel county was a centre of interest. Each congregation had an active committee, supported by municipal and county organizations. The highlight of the programme was an annual convention that drew most of the active teachers of the county for inspiration and instruction. The lessons became the themes of Pidgeon's mid-week addresses, and the elders made Sunday School work their chief concern. Good Sunday School teaching became, although temporarily, a crusading cause.

No local controversies disturbed the calm of the Streetsville ministry, but provincial action against liquor was being seriously discussed. A plebiscite in 1898 and a second referendum shortly afterwards gave large majorities for prohibition. The Liberals became advocates for a while, but took no decisive action. Politicians discovered that few supporters of prohibition would desert their party over the issue, and the temperance leaders grew dispirited.

In January, 1903, a call came to George Pidgeon from Victoria Church, Toronto Junction. It was clear that the new pastorate would not be a repetition of the peaceful experience at Streetsville. Toronto Junction was a congregation in difficulties, situated in a depressed suburb of discouraged railway-

men and factory workers. The challenge of the situation was
effectively presented to Toronto Presbytery, however, by T.
Egerton Shore, minister of Annette Street Methodist Church
at the Junction and a former colleague at Streetsville.

Victoria Church had been founded in a mood of wild
optimism when Toronto Junction was the boom town of the
hour. Tradition has it that the first resolution passed by the
congregation was to build a tower one hundred and forty feet
high, and its other actions were in the same speculative spirit.
Subscriptions were not signed or guaranteed; instead, leading
men of the congregation attached their names to the documents required for financing in the expectation that a single
offering at the opening would pay off the debt. When the
real-estate boom was followed by a crash, the community was
ruined, the church appeared to be doomed, and the guarantors
would be hard put to save their own property from the wreck.

At this point R. L. MacCormack, head of the Conger Coal
Company, went to visit a crippled market gardener named
George Syme, intending to warn him to secure his own property as well as he could from the effect of the church's bank-
ruptcy. Syme was not for pulling out so easily. "Robert," he
said, "we can't get out of it this way. This is God's house. You
stand by me and we'll save the church." Syme immediately
raised one thousand dollars for the church by mortgaging his
own farm, and under the leadership of MacCormack and
others the congregation was able to come to an arrangement
with the loan company.

Although the immediate crisis had passed, the congregation
was left with a heavy burden of debt and a pitifully small
income. In 1902, for example, the average weekly income was
thirty-five dollars to pay a minister, maintain a white elephant
of a building, and retire a debt of over twenty-five thousand
dollars. The effort wrecked the pastorate of J. W. Rae, an

accomplished orator and a recognized leader in the Sunday School movement. Failing to rally the congregation, he had left some months before Pidgeon was called. Fortunately the income of the church soon began to rise, a fact Dr. Pidgeon attributes to returning prosperity.

The new minister was scarcely settled in his congregation when the liquor issue was raised. The Reverend Egerton Shore was at times a sensationalist, and when, early in 1903, he preached a sizzling sermon on moral conditions in the Junction, there was an immediate stir. Shore called attention to violations of the law against Sunday sales of liquor, a charge that was soon proved in the case of every local hotel but one. He attacked with special vigour a gambling house just outside Toronto's city limits.

Shore's immediate object was to demand enforcement of the existing law. Provincial legislation permitted the closing of all bars by local option, however, and before long the local ministerial association was pressing for a vote. One of the leaders in the movement was the Anglican rector, F. H. DuVernet, who was the senior minister of the community and later became bishop of Caledonia in northern British Columbia. DuVernet was not a supporter of prohibition, but he agreed with Pidgeon's argument that cutting down opportunities would reduce drunkenness and provide more income to workers' families. The campaign succeeded, and local merchants soon reported improved business. Indeed, the financial argument was especially effective at that time, and it was sometimes pushed home in colourful ways. In one community the temperance forces got up two petitions. One, signed by practically all the merchants, testified that local option had helped business. The other, urging that taking liquor away had damaged his business, was signed by the undertaker alone.

The evangelistic ferment so evident in Canadian cities

during the first decade of this century was especially marked at Toronto Junction, which had attracted many young people from country districts. Preaching was in great demand, and Pidgeon's interest in evangelism made him eager to seize every possible opportunity. The tradition in those days was for the morning congregation to consist of the faithful core of church members, and so the sermons tended to be expository and thoughtful. In the evenings, young people crowded the church. Dr. Pidgeon recalls that he never had congregations so eager or so responsive, and that even in the darkest days of financial embarrassment church attendance was never a problem.

Among young people the Bible class was in its heyday. The congregation at Toronto Junction had large classes for each sex, led by W. R. Taylor and Anne Moffatt. Taylor, then a student at Knox College, proved to be an especially able assistant. The single young men who had flocked into the Junction had many problems, both intellectual and personal, and Taylor was prepared to grapple with their questions until the early hours of the morning.

Pidgeon still maintained his interest in the International Sunday School Lessons. In 1906 he was asked by the Toronto *Globe* to makes these lessons the basis of weekly articles, and so began a series that was to continue for many years. The family that owned the *Globe* eventually developed premillennial ideas, with the result that in 1923 a more sympathetic commentator took over the column. The series was taken up, however, by the Winnipeg *Free Press* for its *Prairie Farmer* and by the *Kings County Record* of Sussex, New Brunswick. The last article of the series appeared on July 30, 1960.

The campaign against liquor that had begun as a project of the Toronto Junction ministerial association soon spread throughout Ontario, and Pidgeon was frequently called upon to lend his support. One of the early successes of local option was at Owen Sound, where the economic argument once again carried a good deal of weight. Soon, however, the field of action shifted to provincial politics. Arguing that a law against a cherished habit could only be enforced with clear public support, Premier J. P. Whitney had an amendment passed requiring a three-fifths majority before local option could become effective. Temperance forces regarded this action as an intolerable intervention on the side of evil, although they acknowledged that no premier had ever been more co-operative in enforcing prohibition wherever it went into effect.

The methods of temperance advocates were not always well chosen. Dr. Pidgeon describes one occasion when he and a Methodist colleague were allowed to put their case to Whitney. Pidgeon argued calmly for the right of municipalities to outlaw liquor if they wished. The other turned his back on Whitney and harangued the spectators. This was no good, Dr. Pidgeon recalls, for Whitney could shout louder than any Methodist preacher.

Looking around for an effective answer to political obstruction, Pidgeon and his allies determined upon national action by the churches. The Methodists had, in 1902, established a Department of Temperance and Moral Reform, and the result had been to intensify the campaign for prohibition. Likeminded Presbyterians now began to work for a similar organization. In the spring of 1907, Pidgeon sent letters to R. A. (later Sir Robert) Falconer of Halifax, C. W. Gordon (Ralph Connor) of Winnipeg and R. J. Wilson of Vancouver, urging them to persuade their presbyteries to ask the General Assembly of 1907 for a new board. All responded enthusiastically, although Falconer warned on behalf of cautious Maritimers that the "social" aspects of the new department should not be emphasized. A number of presbyteries duly sent overtures, and the Assembly set up a standing committee on "Temperance and other Moral and Social Reforms." This unfortunate title was soon to give way to others only slightly less awkward: "Moral and Social Reform" in 1908, "Social Service and Evangelism" in 1911. George Pidgeon was named convener of the new board. Dr. J. G. Shearer, who in the previous year had persuaded Parliament to pass the Lord's Day Act, became secretary.

During the next two years a great deal of Pidgeon's time was devoted to the promotion of the new board. Money was the most urgent problem. In those days the Presbyterian Church in Canada had no unified budget, and the financing of the board was the responsibility of its supporters. Congregations were urged to accept allocations, and for the chairman this meant a constant stream of letters to officials and key pastors.

Stewart Crysdale, the author of *The Industrial Struggle and Protestant Ethics in Canada,* recalls that in tracing the origins of social concern among Canadian churchmen he kept coming upon the name of George Pidgeon. This prominence, surprising in view of Pidgeon's relative lack of interest in economics and politics, points to the evangelical background of much Canadian social radicalism. Searching for the source of Pidgeon's social interest, one is led back to the Gaspé revivals of the 1880's. Pidgeon was essentially an evangelist who saw how relevant was a favourable environment to the success of his preaching, and he therefore sought to change the environment. There were others like him: William Meikle and his Maritime converts, a group of students at Queen's who after a season of revival demanded the reformation of national life, Methodist prohibitionists who were later to swing to the left. The Canadian custom of associating social service with evangelism goes back a long way.

4. *Westminster Hall*

Westminster Hall was in 1909 one of the most ambitious colleges of the Presbyterian Church in Canada. It was unworthily housed in a made-over frame dwelling in Vancouver's fashionable but makeshift west end, but in almost every other respect it gave the impression of being somewhat larger than life.

The principal, Dr. John A. Mackay, was the centre of the excitement. Called in 1908 from a Montreal pastorate, he quickly caught the expansionist fever native to the Pacific coast. Convinced that the course of empire was moving infallibly westwards, he was able in turn to persuade men of money that British Columbia's material development required as its spiritual complement a major Presbyterian seminary. In time his ambitions reached beyond the theological college, Plans for a university at Point Grey began to take shape, and Mackay seemed to many a logical choice for its first president. Dr. Henry Esson Young, the provincial minister of education, was committed to him, and he was ready for the call. Mackay was to lose the appointment and eventually leave the province a disappointed man, for some influential people who respected his ability feared the political consequences of appointing an ecclesiastic. In 1909, however, such reverses were far in the future, and the prospects seemed unlimited.

Among its teachers, too, the college counted an array of names that could have been matched by no other Canadian seminary. There was never more than a skeleton staff of

41

permanent teachers, but the college managed very well by holding most of its classs while other institutions were on vacation. By offering classes during the summer, Westminster Hall achieved two important advantages. Students were free to do pastoral work in the winter season, when church activities were at their height. Then, in the summer, overseas scholars on vacation could be lured by the prospect of mountain scenery and a mild climate. Among those who came were some of the leading theologians of the time: James Denney, Anderson Scott, George Adam Smith, A. E. Garvie, James Stalker, James Moffatt. To older ministers the list will read almost like a Who's Who of the British free churches during the time of their greatest intellectual influence.

The students were not all so exceptional. Some saw in the summer session an opportunity to make up failed classes or to finish their theological course quickly—the latter ambition was speedily foiled by George Pidgeon as registrar. Others, however, were able men who could never have reached ordination apart from the financial support of full-time winter work. On the whole, the student body was an adventurous group, recruited from every part of Canada and eager to build a new cosmopolitan tradition.

Assembled almost by accident in a city unaware of the past, the members of Westminster Hall felt themselves part of an exciting pioneer venture. Its teachers represented the universal tradition of the church. Its location promised a future of sensational growth. Principal Mackay contributed the needed sense of manifest destiny. In the prevailing mood of optimism, all things seemed possible.

In 1908, when the college was looking for its first principal, George Pidgeon was one of those considered. A year later, Mackay persuaded him to become registrar and professor of practical theology. In 1910 the two were joined by W. R.

Taylor as professor of Old Testament language and literature. Taylor, who had been Pidgeon's student assistant at Toronto Junction, proved to be a most popular teacher; he returned east in 1914 to take charge of oriental studies at the University of Toronto and in 1945 to become principal of University College. The other permanent member of the staff was John A. Logan, a pioneer British Columbian pastor who, as college treasurer, contributed an intimate knowledge of local ways as well as a mature pastoral judgment in working with people.

The Westminster Hall schedule compelled an unusual rhythm of college work. Throughout the summer Pidgeon carried on classes in homiletics, in the conduct of worship and in pastoral work. He also offered a course on current social conditions and the church's attitude to them. During April and June his load of work was at its peak. The visiting lecturers had not arrived, and their places in the timetable had to be filled by the resident teachers. Most of the visitors were New Testament specialists, so it usually fell to Pidgeon to introduce the students through word studies to the passages that would be dealt with during the summer. The winters would be relatively free for preaching and other extracurricular work, but in those expansive days there were usually many college tasks. The teachers were spared involvement in the strenuous task of money-raising, which Mackay himself looked after. Pidgeon was a member of the committee that selected the future site of Union College, however, and this responsibility kept him in close touch with those who were laying out the new campus of the University of British Columbia at Point Grey.

Pidgeon found the college atmosphere congenial. He liked working with students, although some of the older men attracted to Westminster Hall felt that they had little to learn about the practical aspects of church work. He formed warm friendships with some of the distinguished visitors. His home became a social centre for students and lecturers alike. One senses, however, that he was a student rather than a scholar, a teacher and adviser who loved books but did not live for them.

The Pidgeons and their growing family succumbed readily to the notorious charms of Vancouver. Near their home was English Bay with its bathing beach and its roller-skating rink. George Pidgeon often took his wife and children there, introducing them to the water and to the marine life along its edge. Recalling perhaps his boyhood among the log-drivers of the Cascapedia, he took readily to the sea and communicated his delight to those around him. Soon Alice and Arch were exploring English Bay in a huge rowboat, while the family would travel together on longer excursions to Kitsilano or around Prospect Point to Deadman's Bay and along the Hastings shore. On one unforgettable expedition the rowboat was caught in the rip-tide at the Lions Gate, and the oars could be held in the locks only with great difficulty. When still water was finally gained near the shore, the preacher was typically busy conceiving a useful sermon illustration.

A favourite family outing was by ferry to North Vancouver, then by streetcar and on foot to the Capilano suspension bridge. Once across the shaking bridge, one could walk along a flume to the upper canyon, now partially flooded, but then affording a breathtaking view unknown to most Vancouver residents. As the family looked down on the scene, the preacher thought how readily man passes up hidden beauty, especially if a little difficulty is involved—and another illustration was filed for use.

In Vancouver, as in Streetsville, there was time for family concerns. Helen, the second daughter and third child, took her place in the circle. In 1911, Leslie Pidgeon became the minister of St. John's Church in the west end. Crowded with the leaders of Vancouver's society, St. John's was then the strongest Presbyterian congregation in the city. George often preached for his brother, taking services for an entire winter while Leslie finished his arts course at Queen's.

One winter the family was able to visit Britain for study and new contacts. Most of the time was spent in Edinburgh, where Pidgeon was allowed to attend James Seth's lectures to honour students in ethics. The Scottish pulpit was at the height of its power, and no doubt lessons were learned from preachers of the order of Alexander Whyte and J. R. P. Sclater. There were also visits to Oxford and Cambridge. At Oxford, the Pidgeons met James Murray, then busily engaged in editing the *Oxford Dictionary*. In Cambridge, they were entertained by Anderson Scott of Westminster College, their own guest lecturer of the previous summer.

During the British Columbia period, Pidgeon was more deeply involved than ever in the movement for moral reform. His duties at the college included a course on social ethics, his winters allowed time for extracurricular activities, and to one of his temperament and beliefs, the local situation cried out for action. British Columbia still retained some of the features of a raw frontier society: vice was more open and more brazen than in eastern Canada. On the other hand, Vancouver was taking on the airs of a modern city, and saloon toughs were giving way to big-time operators. Dives that in Toronto would still have solicited business furtively were on the west coast almost smugly accepted as elements of local colour.

In a community where virtue and vice confronted one another so openly, the lines of battle were sharply and frankly drawn, and the protagonists expressed themselves with a candour that surprises even today. Politics was a matter not of left and right but of dirty and clean. To leaders of the churches, moral issues usually seemed clear enough; action was more often inhibited by a lack of courage than by a lack of certainty.

One incident that took place at Nelson was typical of the open warfare of the period. E. S. Logie, the Presbyterian minister there, had been engaged in a campaign to rid the city of its red-light district. Feeling had mounted, and when a meeting was called for the town hall, it was rumoured that a gang of young punks was organizing to prevent the minister from speaking. He insisted on going through with his plan, and when he entered the hall there was a group right before him. A local doctor was known to be making a reputation for his treatment of venereal diseases. So, quickly sizing up the situation, Logie began, "I have been told that a number of young men who are indebted to Dr. R. for medical treatment have planned to keep me from speaking. I hope it isn't true." He was able to deliver, without interruption, a speech that spared no feelings.

The national chairman of the new Presbyterian Board of Moral and Social Reform, in 1909 Pidgeon became president of the Christian Social Council of British Columbia. Throughout his tenure at Westminster Hall, he held these two strategic positions. He also became, in 1913, a member of the executive of the Social Service Council of Vancouver. In the course of his duties he interviewed civic officials and cabinet ministers, and got to know intimately leaders of other churches, including the Roman Catholic.

This last contact was one that Pidgeon came to value greatly. On a visit to Vancouver, Dr. Shearer took him to visit Archbishop Neil MacNeil, a Highlander from Cape Breton. Later, when a crank had introduced an anti-Roman resolution in presbytery, MacNeil called for Pidgeon. MacNeil was polite but wanted to know what was back of such resolutions. "They talk as if they think we have no feelings," he complained. The explanation must have been satisfactory, for Pidgeon continued to be called in when similar situations arose.

The first issue to be raised in Vancouver was law enforcement. When Pidgeon went to British Columbia, he found horse racing being carried on without restriction. This astonished him, for Shearer had succeeded in obtaining an amendment to the federal act restricting horse racing to certain times. Vancouver had a shadowy moral reform organization at the time, but it was doing very little. Pidgeon revived it to deal with the crisis of gambling at the tracks.

The much more serious issue was prostitution. The city's red-light district was concentrated on Alexander Street, where brothel operators had been largely exempt from prosecution. Inside information claimed this immunity was granted by the provincial attorney-general, W. J. Bowser, who stood for a wide-open province. Pidgeon learned that on one occasion the local magistrate had begun to enforce the law, but that Bowser himself had come over from Victoria to stop him. Enforcement was a local responsibility, so the moral reform group demanded a conference with the city council.

The mayor opened the meeting by attacking one of the ministers who on the previous Sunday had denounced the civic authorities for failure to enforce the law against prostitution. Dr. R. J. Wilson of St. Andrew's Church, who had preached the offending sermon, listened in silence until the mayor had finished.

Then he asked, "Have you given orders for the enforcement of law against commercialized vice?"

"Do you mean Alexander Street?" the mayor asked in turn.

"Yes."

"I have not," the mayor acknowledged.

"Then," said Dr. Wilson, "my statement stands."

In this unpromising atmosphere, Pidgeon presented the delegation's case, but without immediate result.

Before long the campaign was extended to include other issues besides narrowly moral ones. Churchmen who urged enforcement of laws against prostitution were constantly asked by the authorities, "What provision have you made for those poor girls when we enforce the law against them?" Shearer responded by organizing rescue homes in several of the larger cities, and Miss Marie-Christine Ratté, a French-Canadian convert with first-hand knowledge of slum conditions, began a remarkable mission to social outcasts. The churches were being forced to take positive social action to give weight to their moral campaign.

Economic questions also began to demand attention. In the rural areas people were more indignant about the price of land than about specific moral issues. Bowser had a bad reputation for favouring speculators, and settlers began to complain that when new areas were opened the land grabbers were always there first. In one fertile valley, made accessible by a new railway line, settlers were reported to be clustered on hillsides while speculators held out for higher prices on the fertile bottom-land they had secured in advance. Soon Pidgeon found himself addressing meetings throughout the Kootenays on the subject.

The nature of the campaign was imperceptibly changing, with moral reform shading into economic radicalism. Those who had begun by denouncing unrighteousness found themselves challenged to provide an environment favourable to righteousness. Limited success in enforcing existing laws led to demands for new laws, and eventually to a more thorough-going analysis of the whole social order. Proponents of personal morality and of economic justice were further linked by the need of joint action against common enemies. Behind brothel and land-grab alike there was the wealth created by the new urbanism.

Inevitably, the reform movement began to split into two

wings. After attending a Social Service Congress in Ottawa in early 1914, Pidgeon was able to report:

Our methods often differ, and so do our views. Formerly such differences divided us hopelessly and forbade co-operation. Now we realize that we all hate the one foe, that we are all working toward the same end, and that our agreements are deeper and broader far than our differences.*

For the moment, as moralists and socialists shared the inspiration of a harmonious conference, the various wings of the reform movement might seem closer together than ever before. After 1914, however, the tension between reformer and radical became steadily more pronounced, and the old moral crusade lost much of its fire. Pidgeon would always retain his interest in what would later be called "the evangelization of Canadian life," but henceforth moral reform as a cause would absorb less and less of his energy.

Even more satisfying to Pidgeon than his public adventures, perhaps, were the opportunities he had for direct evangelism during the long winter vacations. There was scarcely a Sunday when he did not preach, and on several occasions he led special missions to cities in the interior. In one of these missions, at Chilliwack in the Fraser Valley, he was assisted by a number of his students from the college. It pleased him greatly that he could share with them the practical application of the methods of sermon instruction and delivery he had taught them in the classroom.

Although Pidgeon was never a sensationalist in either the style or the content of his preaching, one feels oneself surrounded by signs and portents as he is followed on his missions through British Columbia.

At Nelson, a girl was lying dangerously ill—hopelessly ill, according to her doctor. But her parents persisted in the belief that their prayers for her recovery would be granted. Asked

---

The Westminster Hall Magazine, Vol. V, No. 2 (March, 1914), p. 13.

by concerned neighbours to prepare the parents for what seemed inevitable, Pidgeon preached from John 15: 7 a sermon on "The Prayer of Faith" that was to be one of his best known sermons. He tried to show from Scripture and experience that God responds to prayer that is "driven home to his heart," and that although his response might be a denial it might also be effective. The parents thanked him and kept on praying. A year later one of the first to welcome him on another visit to Nelson was this girl, just in from an evening of coasting. "But the mother who prayed her through was gone."

At Penticton, a young woman sang solos to bring home the appeal of Pidgeon's sermons. After one such appeal, her voice broke in the middle of her song, and the congregation became tense with worry. She regained her self-command, finished her song, and in a few minutes turned in a card recording her decision for Christ. Dr. Pidgeon comments, "That series should have been continued. If so, the whole community would have been moved."

There are no stories of miracles. Everywhere, however, the preacher found evidence of God's working around him and through him. Such examples were woven into his sermons, and he preached in the constant expectation of marvels that might follow.

Dr. Pidgeon recalls that his years in British Columbia were among the happiest of his life. But by the time the First World War had broken out, some of the excitement of pioneering had worn off. The economy of British Columbia collapsed in 1914, and many of the moral issues raised by the preceding boom became less urgent. Students began to enlist, and potential students were too preoccupied to feel the attraction of summer courses on the west coast. Many of Principal Mackay's dreams had been shattered, and there was less now for a second-in-command to do. Westminster Hall would have to wait for its promised future.

5. *Return to the Pastorate*

Many of Dr. Pidgeon's recollections are preserved in the form
of notes typed from dictation. Reading these notes, one is made
aware of the author's preoccupation with his development as
a preacher. At each stage of the narrative he records his
progress in meticulous detail. On his first mission field he
began by writing his sermons in full but taking into the pulpit
only key words for each sentence. Experience at Darling led
him to try preaching without notes, and at Waterford the
experiment became a settled practice. At Victoria Church in
Montreal he made the radical innovation of writing out only
the morning sermon in full. At Toronto Junction he cultivated the evening service. Streetsville and the International
Sunday School Lessons taught him to build each sermon
around a single theme, "explained, illustrated and applied." In
British Columbia he became deeply concerned about life
situations, and these found their way into his sermons. 'It is
scarcely possible to doubt that at all stages of his ministry
his sense of vocation found its most satisfying expression in
the pulpit.

Although he has always been a student as well as a preacher,
the student in him consistently served the preacher. He was
never, indeed, one of those homiletical scavengers who ran-
sack Scriptures and literature for novel texts and telling illustrations. He customarily chose for exposition biblical passages
that had figured in his own religious development, and his

literary allusions reflected his enjoyment of the classics. Always, however, he directed his study into fields likely to be homiletically fertile. In his theological studies he concentrated on the language and text of the New Testament. In his secular reading he was attracted to writers of religious and moral purpose, from Spenser to the eminent Victorians.

Even Pidgeon's public activities were essentially extensions of his pulpit ministry. At Streetsville he learned that for him the secret of effective preaching was to select a central idea of the Christian faith and to apply it to the lives of his people. He was already insisting in Montreal West that application must be in deeds as well as in words. In tracing Pidgeon's career, it is not easy to distinguish clearly between moral and social campaigns and evangelistic missions. He would not regard the distinction as important, for both were expressions of a single ministry. At no point, however, did he doubt which aspect of his ministry was primary: he was a reforming preacher, not a preaching reformer.

To one whose heart was in his preaching, a professor's chair at Westminster Hall offered abundant opportunities. In the classroom he was able to teach future ministers the techniques of sermon preparation and delivery. On Sundays he was almost always in the pulpit, and the winters were free for sustained campaigns of evangelism. It was a special joy to go on tour with students and to see them apply their acquired techniques in situations where souls were at stake. Canadian theological colleges have always been much closer to the day-by-day life of the church than their American counterparts. Pidgeon thoroughly enjoyed his years at Westminster Hall, and he has never suggested that he felt himself shut off in an ivory tower.

But a preacher cannot long be satisfied without a pulpit of his own. He will constantly be planning series of sermons, devising improved orders of service, applying texts to the needs of an imagined congregation. As he taught methods of sermon preparation, Pidgeon must often have hankered to put new ideas into practice himself. A visiting lecturer introduced him to the writings of the American frontier evangelist Asa Mahan, and he was able to pick up a copy of Mahan's sermons in a London bookshop. The result was to rekindle his interest in a form of preaching that had shaped his earliest religious experience. He found in Mahan a depth lacking in many better-known evangelists, and his nostalgia for the pulpit was increased. Mrs. Pidgeon encouraged his growing desire to return to regular preaching. She missed in the college the close personal contacts she had known at Streetsville and Toronto Junction, and she felt that her husband had a talent for pastoral work that was not being fully used in academic life. If Westminster Hall had continued to provide the stimulating environment of its early years, a return to the pastorate might have been indefinitely postponed. But as students left for the forces, the Pidgeons began to grow restless.

In 1915, Bloor Street Church in Toronto was looking for an associate to its minister, Dr. W. G. Wallace. The office of associate minister is peculiar to Presbyterianism. Reformed polity as it developed in Scotland made no place for assistantships. No matter how large the congregation or how onerous the work, the consistent Scottish mind could not conceive the possibility of inducting a minister without entrusting to him responsibility for the cure of souls. Where, through age or infirmity, a minister seemed near the end of his pastorate, however, the custom arose of calling an associate who would preside jointly over the congregation with the right of sole succession. Presbyterian logic was satisfied, for the associate was inducted into at least a share of the responsibility for a congregation.

Bloor Street Church was founded in 1887 to serve Presbyterians in Toronto's university area. The congregation met at first in Knox College, where its services were led by the various professors. From the first, the congregation thought in large terms of its future. It built in the Annex a church that must have seemed beyond its immediate means or needs, and it called a minister who was regarded as one of the promising young men of the time. Dr. Wallace, Pidgeon's only predecessor at Bloor Street, had in the course of a twenty-five-year ministry built up a strong neighbourhood congregation. Essentially a pastor, he had made sure of the loyalty and cohesion of his people by assiduous visiting and solid preaching. He lacked the intellectual brilliance that would have held the attention of university students, but he cultivated progressive leadership within his congregation. Bloor Street was one of the first congregations in Canada to support its own missionary overseas. It shared the enthusiasm of the period for new methods and programmes of Christian education, and it had a fine corps of leaders.

Bloor Street in 1915 presented an attractive challenge to a rising preacher. The Annex was losing its old homogeneity, and the congregation was beginning to scatter throughout the city. On the other hand, the northward march of Toronto was making the church's situation more strategic than ever. Bloor Street Church was becoming a down-town congregation in a day when roomers and visitors to the city still had the habit of church attendance. Students were concentrated in the area and would respond to evangelistic preaching. Best of all, the congregation was prepared to provide facilities and leadership for the shepherding of those who might be attracted.

In March, 1915, Pidgeon preached at Bloor Street with a view to a call. The clinching argument in favour of returning to the pastorate was his conviction that as minister of a university area congregation he would be able to provide a more useful ministry even to students than had been possible in the college setting. In September he was inducted as associate minister, on the understanding that he should preach every second Sunday morning and conduct all the evening services.

On the basis of his earlier experience, Pidgeon expected to make the evening service the focus of his ministry at Bloor Street. He was able to develop continuous series of sermons and to preach them in a crowded church. After a few weeks, however, the prolonged absence of Dr. Wallace on a honeymoon trip in Europe gave him temporary responsibility for both services. He soon discovered that at Bloor Street the morning service was primary both for congregation and for students. Perhaps the evening service, so popular during the early decades of urbanization in Canada, was imperceptibly beginning its long decline. In any event, he was henceforth to concentrate more attention on the thoughtful pastoral discourse associated with morning worship.

One assignment in the summer of 1916 was to have unexpected and varied consequences. The Reverend Charles W. Bishop had been a colleague of Vancouver days. Now, as head of the Canadian YMCA, he invited Pidgeon to lead the Bible studies in its summer programme at Geneva Park on Lake Couchiching. The family was thus enabled to have a summer vacation in the country, and Pidgeon himself found ample time for relaxation. One unplanned result was to revive an earlier passion for canoeing. Arch was the first to discover the area's suitability for exploration by canoe, and on one occasion he set off on a trip alone. The pain of missing the fun was so great that the father resolved not to be left behind again, and the summer canoe trip became an annual highlight. Several times the pair followed the Severn River down to Georgian Bay and up again to Lake Couchiching.

A more serious result of the YMCA assignment was the continuation of the Bible study in a different setting. A group of YMCA secretaries at Geneva Park had arranged that Pidgeon should lead them in special classes. At the end of the season some of them were reluctant to see the project die. They accordingly organized the Toronto Business Men's Noon-day Bible Club, a group that still meets regularly in a private room at Simpson's Arcadian Court. The club met for four months during the winter. During the first year or two Pidgeon was the sole leader. Later, various ministers were invited to take sessions of a month or a season, but he always maintained his close association with the group. Much of the material used in two of these series was later published in *The Vicarious Life* (1945) and *The Indwelling Christ* (1948).

The early days of the Bloor Street ministry, happy in many ways, were darkened by the shadow of war. Pidgeon had always had a special interest in work for young people, but at Bloor Street the young men were gone when he arrived. He wrote letters to them, heard of them on pastoral visits, and sometimes had to break to parents the news of their deaths. Having never met them, however, he began to feel them to be ghostly presences symbolizing the incompleteness of his personal understanding of his congregation.

Those left behind in a war are apt to experience a peculiar sense of loneliness. Perhaps it was this, and the possibility of meeting some of his own unknown boys, that made Pidgeon so responsive to an opportunity to visit the front. The YMCA, known to servicemen today chiefly for its recreational facilities, retained then a double interest in evangelism and social service. The social centres were well looked after, but some in the Canadian branch of the organization felt that the evangelistic side of the work needed reinforcement. It was therefore decided in 1917 to send a preacher to each of the three divisions at the front. W. A. Cameron was to look after the first division, George Pidgeon the second, and John McNeill the third. Their instructions were to hold evangelistic meetings as close to the battle line as possible.

From September, 1917, to May, 1918, Pidgeon preached to the Canadian troops in France and England. From Canada he proceeded directly to the battle area, where men were brought to his meetings from the trenches with mud still on their tunics. It was a sobering and searing experience to move directly from the secure comfort of Toronto into the company of men hardened by several years of battle. He would not readily forget occasions when he was catapulted into the dark on the side of a motorcycle, or when he walked calmly with a friend within the range of German fire. There was a pleasant side, too, as he met some of the young men of Bloor Street who had hitherto been merely names on a list. He did his evangelistic work conscientiously, finding that in the urgency of the battle situation the direct message succeeded where the fuller explanation failed.

Pidgeon returned from Europe with the expectation of continuing as Bloor Street's associate minister. Wallace immediately informed him, however, that he had decided to step aside so that the younger man could take complete charge, and in September he resigned. Pidgeon was now sole minister, free to introduce new methods after decades of a very personal and pastoral type of ministry.

Pidgeon's first concern was with the organization of the congregation. Wallace had kept all the records in his head. At his associate's induction, Wallace was able to introduce him to the entire congregation, hesitating over only one or two names. When sick calls were to be made, he could give from memory lists of names and street numbers. This technique, however admirable in a neighbourhood congregation, could not be applied to the shifting population of Bloor Street at the end of the first war.

A landmark was the appointment of Ethel K. Ross as

secretary. Miss Ross came from the headquarters of International Rotary at Washington, but had previously been secretary to Leslie Pidgeon at Augustine Church, Winnipeg. She brought order to the files and to congregational life, combining a keen sense of responsibility with sympathy for those who especially needed the church's help. Her service at Bloor Street was to last thirty years, her retirement in 1948 coinciding with Pidgeon's own.

Other significant appointments followed. Soon there was a deaconess to assist with work among women, and in October, 1919, the Reverend C. M. Wright came as the first of several directors of Christian education. These appointments were symptomatic of a spirit of innovation in church life that was typical of the post-war period. Pidgeon experimented with what were later to be called visual aids. In 1920 a junior congregation and kindergarten services were begun. Other developments indicated the public spirit of the congregation. Bloor Street members gave generous leadership to the activities of St. Christopher's House in down-town Toronto, and the congregation supported a series of paid women workers there. When, at the end of the war, Principal Alfred Gandier of Knox called for a church-wide thank-offering, a group at Bloor Street contributed about $100,000.

Despite the exacting demands of a new and large pastorate, Pidgeon continued to find time for contacts beyond his own congregation. His ministry to students and business men took a great deal of effort. He took a keen interest in civic affairs, and likes to recall that his close friendship with Rabbi Ferdinand M. Isserman of the old Holy Blossom Synagogue was one of the first of its kind in the city. His convenership of the Board of Social Service and Evangelism lapsed when that board was absorbed into the Board of Home Missions, but in 1917 he was appointed convener of the latter. In 1918 he became president of the Social Service Council of Canada, later heading its Ontario branch. National interests remained, although for a few years no issue seems to have kindled his customary fire.

As early as 1913, still a professor at Westminster Hall, Pidgeon had associated himself with an ambitious enterprise in publishing. A number of Canadian scholars and church-men projected a Canadian Library of Religious Literature, originally intended to consist of twenty volumes. Pidgeon, as chief editor, arranged for their publication by Hodder and Stoughton. The outbreak of war interrupted work after a single volume had appeared, and when the war was over, almost insuperable obstacles intervened. The publisher gloomily predicted that rising prices would soon make the production of books forever impossible, and one self-assured author held out for a starting royalty of twenty-five per cent. Several volumes were finally issued by the reluctant publisher, and young Arch Pidgeon began his business career by hawk-ing the set.

It was in the pulpit, however, that George Pidgeon's powers were more and more being concentrated. The author can recall from his childhood the accepted opinion that Pidgeon was "Canada's greatest preacher." That reputation was earned only by constant intellectual and spiritual effort to preach well. In a sermon delivered near the end of his ministry, he indicated how arduous the effort had been:

There is no harder taskmaster than the ambition to excel in the pulpit. No slave-driver ever drove his victims as merci-lessly as the art to which one's life is dedicated. She calls for thorough preparation every time you enter her sanctuary, but she requires more than preparation. There is a mystic way into her holy of holies which only the elect can find; she has meanings hidden in every text, or theme, which she discloses only to those who love her so that they cannot but follow her to the end.*

---

*"Fifty Years Trying," a sermon preached in Bloor Street United Church, Toronto, May 28, 1944.

6. Enlisted for Church Union

Long before George Pidgeon had begun his ministry, Canadian Presbyterians were giving serious thought to proposals for union with other denominations. The Presbyterian Church in Canada was itself the result of a series of unions crowned in 1875 by the coming together of the four remaining segments. Each union had significantly been made the occasion for prophecies of wider unions yet to come.

One of those who anticipated such a greater union was Dr. John Cook, principal and professor of theology at Morrin College while Pidgeon was a student there. At the time of his election as first moderator of the Presbyterian Church in Canada, Cook wrote:

Far larger union is, I trust, in store for the Churches of Christ even in Canada than that which is in effect this day. This is but a small step to the union which our Lord's intercessory prayer seems to contemplate. . . . I look for union in the future before which the present union, blessed and auspicious though we justly count it, shall appear slight and insignificant. May God hasten it in His time![*]

Principal Grant was already an advocate of wider union. In 1874 he had read in Montreal a paper entitled "The Church of Canada—can such a thing be?" In 1883 and 1884 he wrote two articles on "Church Union in Canada," arguing for union with the Methodists as the first step towards a more inclusive church. MacVicar, at odds with him on many issues, agreed on this one.

---

[*]Quoted by G. C. Pidgeon, *The United Church of Canada* (Toronto, Ryerson, 1950), p. 15.

By 1902, when Pidgeon was still at Streetsville, the first steps towards the formation of The United Church of Canada were taken. As the General Conference of the Methodist Church was meeting in Winnipeg that year, the Presbyterians named three ministers of that city as fraternal delegates. Principal William Patrick, the third to speak, made an impassioned appeal for the unification of Canadian Protestantism. In 1904 Presbyterians, Methodists and Congregationalists began formal discussions of union, and by 1916 the three denominations had voted to unite. Within twelve years—a very short space of time as ecclesiastics measure it—negotiations had advanced to the point where a united church seemed to be on the verge of formation. Only the absence of so many church members at the war compelled delay.

George Pidgeon has long been recognized as one of the outstanding leaders of the movement towards church union. Among Canadians of Presbyterian background, indeed, his name has been more closely connected with the union than any other, and he has received a great deal of the credit—and the blame—for its successful consummation. This prominence relates, however, to the later stages of the movement. In the formative years that led to the decision of the three churches to unite, he played a negligible role.

The features of the church-to-be took their basic shape in the years from 1904 to 1908, as representatives of the three churches hammered out their Basis of Union. A doctrinal statement, a polity and methods of settling ministers were all worked out during this period. Pidgeon was not a member of the committee or of any of the subcommittees that composed the Basis of Union. Apart from a few late and relatively unimportant amendments, he had no part in drafting the constitution of the United Church. In 1916, when the General Assembly of the Presbyterian Church determined upon union by a vote of 406 to 90, he was present to give his support to the project. Up to that time, however, he had not been actively associated with the movement for union.

Dr. Pidgeon has even disclosed that his first overt action on the union issue was on behalf of delay. His hesitation was due partly to reservations about some features of the Basis, but chiefly to his dissatisfaction with the manner in which union was being presented to the people. Principal Patrick, who had been in Canada only two years when he publicly proposed union to the Methodist Conference, continued to give forceful leadership to the movement in its early stages. Never a man to suffer gladly those whom he regarded as fools, Patrick brushed aside with contempt the arguments of any who ventured to oppose him. There was naturally some resentment. Pidgeon himself was disturbed, and, as he travelled across Canada in 1911 in the interests of the Board of Moral and Social Reform, he became aware of a good deal of grass-roots restlessness.

A personal factor intensified Pidgeon's concern. John Mackay, then the young minister of Crescent Street Church, Montreal, made a fiery speech against union at the General Assembly of 1906. He immediately became the recognized leader of the anti-union forces, and maintained his stand while principal of Westminster Hall. At the Assembly of 1910, an hour-long attack threatened to carry the day until Principal Patrick took the floor and dismissed him cavalierly as a stripling unworthy of a serious hearing. Dr. Pidgeon credits Patrick's logic with saving the union movement, but he resented the indignity offered to a principal whom he greatly admired.

At the Assembly of 1911, therefore, Pidgeon was one of a group that arranged a conference between the leading supporters and opponents of union. When the attempt to

mediate failed, he retreated into the background again. He
was satisfied that the church was doing all in its power to conciliate the anti-unionist minority, but he was still not a conspicuous enthusiast for union. No one would have selected
him as the person most likely to be remembered as the father
of church union, although he had long been a leader in other
aspects of church life.

Then, in 1917, Pidgeon became convener of the church's
Board of Home Missions. The work of social service and
evangelism had recently been entrusted to this board, and it
may be safely assumed that Pidgeon was selected for his new
task as a prominent supporter of moral reform. The immediate
result, however, was to put him in close touch with the church
life of the new frontiers of the north and west. The ultimate
result was to put him in the forefront of the movement for
union.

To appreciate the strategic relation of the Board of Home
Missions to the union movement, we need to recall a vital
chapter in Canadian church history. Dr. H. H. Walsh has
called attention to the anxiety with which all denominations
watched the settlement of the west.* The first wave of settlers
who poured into the prairies with the Canadian Pacific Railway were largely of British stock. Many were from eastern
Canada, and practically all had established church connections. To hold them, the churches needed only to send
ministers and build sanctuaries. In the fluid conditions of
the frontier, however, many would respond to the overtures
of the first denomination that offered its services. Failure to
move swiftly could mean virtual exclusion from the new
empire and a significant loss of national stature. Despite
outward friendliness among the churches, there was a great
deal of frenzied competition, especially in the more strategic

*The Christian Church in Canada (Toronto, Ryerson, 1956), Ch. 18.

centres. Dr. James Robertson, the energetic Presbyterian superintendent of missions, was frankly competitive in his attitude and frankly suspicious of Methodist tactics. His mission was to build Presbyterian churches, and to build them before others built theirs. In many cases he succeeded.

By the turn of the century, however, denominational leaders were having second thoughts. For one thing, the geography of the prairies offered little encouragement to ecclesiastical rivalry. Wheat farming calls for large acreages, with farms measured in quarter-sections and sections. Rural areas, even when fully settled, supported populations too sparse to maintain redundant itinerants. Most of the towns remained small, far too small to make room for several prosperous churches. Besides, the second wave of immigration was much less homogenous than the first, bringing fewer Ontario Protestants and more Ukrainian Uniates. The denominations were being faced not merely with a problem of church extension but with a genuine missionary challenge, and churches have always been more willing to co-operate in converting outsiders than in rounding up supporters. Meanwhile, ministerial supply was becoming an ever more pressing problem. Robertson and his contemporaries had been tireless in recruiting likely candidates in Britain, but this source of reinforcements could not be milked indefinitely. Eastern Canada was pressed to provide men, and only in the triangle comprising southern Ontario and Montreal did congregations contribute more to home mission funds than they drew from them.*

In 1902, the year James Robertson died and Principal Patrick proposed organic union, the Presbyterian and Methodist churches appointed a committee to find means of preventing overlapping in the west. The denominations were at last

---

*So Pidgeon concluded for the Presbyterians shortly after the First World War; and the situation among other denominations was probably no better. *The United Church of Canada,* p. 25.

giving up their dreams of establishing separate empires on the prairies, were indeed admitting that the maintenance of a multitude of scattered preaching points was straining their meagre resources. For the first few years co-operation was informal and unsystematic. It was agreed that so far as possible each denomination should keep out of areas already served by the other, but neither showed any inclination to give up key centres.

The change from Robertson's day was great, however, and several writers have insisted that it was made possible only by the fact that negotiations for union were being seriously undertaken.* Concluding in the course of these discussions that there was no fundamental difference between them in doctrine or practice, each church found itself able with a good conscience to trust its members to the supervision of the other.

Although the first ventures in co-operation were brought about by agreement among home mission boards, westerners soon took the initiative themselves in breaking down denominational barriers. Mission boards were anxious to prevent the waste of men and money; the people, resenting compulsory transfer to other denominations, wanted community churches they could call their own. The publication of the completed draft of the proposed Basis of Union in 1908 gave them their inspiration and their opportunity. By November of that year a church was organized on the terms of the Basis at Melville, Saskatchewan, and others quickly followed. These churches looked forward to the day when they would be incorporated into The United Church of Canada. Meanwhile they regarded all delay with impatience. When the Presbyterian General Assembly of 1912 postponed

*C. E. Silcox, *Church Union in Canada* (New York, Institute of Social and Religious Research, 1933), p. 230; E. H. Oliver, *The Winning of the Frontier* (Toronto, United Church Publishing House, 1930), p. 248; Pidgeon, *op. cit.*, p. 58.

action to conciliate dissidents, partly at the instigation of a group that included Pidgeon, there was a new rash of local unions. Other unions were the inevitable result of a crisis of supply brought on by the enlistment of ministers and students in the forces, and by the spectacular growth and wide scattering of the prairie population due to the construction of railway branch lines.

The growth of independent union churches soon posed a threat to the parent denominations. Although drawing aid in men and money, community congregations showed little inclination to contribute to mission funds. In many other ways, too, they were cut off from the national fellowships to which their members belonged. The churches organized according to the Basis were fast becoming a new denomination. They called together their own general council, which eventually had three presbyteries and, by 1921, were represented in their own right on the joint union committee. But what if the union should fail to go through? Leaders of all negotiating denominations feared that their western members might secede in a body, and that even prolonged delay might lead to an impatience that would endanger national unity. The fears were not groundless: Dr. S. D. Chown, the general superintendent of the Methodist Church, heard secession warmly debated by members of the Council of the Local Union Churches,* and in 1918 the Saskatchewan Conference of the Methodist Church sent up a memorial proposing union with the Local Union Churches without waiting for the Presbyterians.†

During the later stages of the local union movement, most of the moves of the national churches were defensive. An

---

The Story of Church Union in Canada (Toronto, Ryerson, 1930), p. 48.
†Silcox, *op. cit.*, p. 178.

"Agreement for Co-operation in Home Mission Work," adopted in 1911, provided for joint work under the auspices of one or another denomination. It was relatively successful in Alberta, but Saskatchewan preferred independent union on the Basis. In 1916, recognizing the appeal of the Local Union movement, the churches appointed an advisory council. In 1917 they sponsored the affiliation of union congregations with one denomination or another and, when this met resistance double and even triple affiliation was encouraged. Still the threat of a new denomination remained.

In 1917 the Presbyterian Church of Canada found itself in an embarrassing position. It was already committed to union, but in view of substantial opposition many felt that it would be unfair to proceed further with so many ministers and members absent at the front. Accordingly, Professor James Ballantyne of Knox College started a petition asking that the issue be set aside until the end of the first year after the war. During the truce, however, individual congregations would be allowed to unite with the Assembly's blessing. Many anti-unionists applauded the suggestion, feeling perhaps that the result would be to relax some of the pressure for a broader union. Ballantyne, an elder of Bloor Street Church, asked Pidgeon to sign his petition. Pidgeon declined, saying:

I cannot honourably sign that petition. As chairman of the Board of Home Missions, I know that the moment the General Assembly approves of local unions in affiliation with one or other of the historic churches, mission charges and weaker congregations will rush into Unions all over the land, and I should be charged justly with double dealing if I signed a petition for a truce while head of a Board which will do more to bring Church Union into effect than all other influences put together.[*]

---

[*]*The United Church of Canada,* p. 56.

The Assembly followed Ballantyne's advice, with the results that Pidgeon had foreseen. In a single year 140 congregations in northern Ontario united. By 1922, unions of one kind or another embraced more than a thousand pastoral charges including three thousand worshipping units. Silcox believed that there would have been hundreds more if the churches had been more indulgent. *

Pidgeon had now committed himself to the unionist cause. In 1917 he was appointed to the executive of the Assembly's committee on church union. Within four years of his active enlistment, he had become the official leader of the movement throughout the Presbyterian Church, and he was to maintain that leadership through another four years of bitter conflict.

One naturally wonders how he came so suddenly to play such a crucial role in a movement to which he had previously made so little direct contribution. Some exploration of his motives is essential to an understanding of his significance in the story of church union, and indeed to the telling of that story itself.

Pidgeon was assuredly no last-minute convert to the cause of Christian unity. Temperament and experience predisposed him to it. Historians agree that the religious climate making the discussion of union possible owed a great deal to a series of evangelical movements. These movements fostered a renewal of religious enthusiasm and an urge to social action that flowed readily across denominational boundaries. Presbyterians of evangelical bent found Methodists unusually congenial, for the latter were evangelicals by definition. In Canada the movement for moral reform did much to bring the like-minded of the two denominations together. Pidgeon, like many other Presbyterians, came to regard the Methodists as natural allies in the fight against entrenched social evils.

Church Union in Canada, p. 225.

Union also made a strong appeal to the idealism of the
moral reformers. From the time of Confederation some
leaders had urged that only a church of national dimensions
could impart a Christian character to the new nation. As
industrialization and immigration began to change the face
of Canada, the formation of such a church seemed ever more
urgent. By the turn of the century, church union was a live
option and many of those who rallied around the banner of
evangelism and social service came to regard it as one of the
signs of the coming kingdom of righteousness.

As early as 1899, Pidgeon preached at Streetsville a sermon
on "The Unity of Believers," taking as his text the prayer of
Jesus in John 17: 21 "that they all may be one." The sermon
was part of a series based on the International Sunday School
Lessons; according to his attached notes, it had been delivered
five times by 1903, once in a Methodist church. In it he urged
that churches no longer divided by historic disputes should
unite without delay, adding:

As between our church and the Methodists, for instance, the
doctrinal controversies of the past are dead and no one wants
to resurrect them. . . . I do not believe that old prejudices
will much longer keep two bodies apart in organization who
are drawing closer together in method, mind and spirit every
year.

No doubt it was largely his distaste for Patrick's methods,
and his admiration for Principal Mackay, that prevented
Pidgeon from being a strong partisan of the union movement
in its early years. Then, in 1916, the General Assembly, having
secured the assent of two-thirds of the presbyteries as required
by the so-called Barrier Act, resolved to unite with the Methodist and Congregational churches. Immediately the consummation of union became, in his mind, a moral commitment.
In the years that followed, his sense of moral obligation became steadily stronger.

Pidgeon believed that after 1916 the Presbyterian Church was committed, first of all, to the Methodists and Congregationalists. Once union was contemplated, any delay meant a period of uncertainty during which the freedom of action of all denominations was abridged. Methodists and Congregationalists refrained from laying ambitious plans for expansion. In many areas, too, both denominations willingly surrendered members to union congregations. This was all to the good if the union should take place. If it were to fail, Presbyterians would have to accept responsibility for widespread dislocation. Pidgeon especially admired the restraint of Methodist leaders in the face of attacks on their integrity by Presbyterian anti-unionists, and he felt that everything possible should be done to repay their generosity.

There was also a commitment, he believed, to the local union churches. Members of all denominations had put aside personal preferences to make such unions possible. They had done so in the expectation of wider union, and it would be unfair to put them in a position where they would be cut off from the main stream of national religious life. In his own writings, Pidgeon always laid stress on "the significant fact that not once . . . was it ever suggested that any vital truth or principle was imperilled by leaving their people in charge of a minister of one of the negotiating churches."[*]

Equally important was the commitment of the Presbyterian Church to its own members. If union now failed to take place, those who had supported their church's action would be seriously compromised. Some had entered local unions, while others had been active in bringing them about.

Even more decisive was Pidgeon's conviction that in backing out of union at this stage the Presbyterian Church would be untrue to itself and would forfeit the respect of others. He

---

[*]*Op. cit.*, p. 29.

felt strongly that orderly action through church courts is of the essence of Presbyterian polity. It seemed to him unthinkable that the church should go back on an action that had been regularly determined upon, especially when that action had irreversible effects throughout the country. He could only regard the denial of the right of the church to take such action as rebellion against Presbyterianism.

The church union controversy gave rise to bitter feelings that no one wishes to revive today. To appreciate Pidgeon's position, however, one must recall that to partisans on both sides, intensely moral issues were involved. Pidgeon himself could respect some but not all of the opponents of union. Principal Mackay believed from the beginning that the union movement was a mistake and opposed it doggedly in church courts. Once the church had made its decision, however, he withdrew from the campaign. Pidgeon's admiration for him increased. He could not feel the same about those who not only maintained their opposition but claimed that only they stood in the true Presbyterian heritage. He came to believe that in supporting the union he was upholding the honour of the Presbyterian Church.

Although a moral conviction sufficed to make Pidgeon a determined supporter of union, it was a practical issue that brought him into the field as an ardent warrior on its behalf. The crisis of decision was precipitated by his appointment, in 1917, as convener of the Board of Home Missions. Undoubtedly he had long been aware of the existence of strong union sentiment on the frontier. Now, however, he was directly confronted by the impatience of the west, by its bitterness at delay and by its apparent readiness to adopt extreme measures. He was profoundly shocked by what he saw and heard as he carried out his new duties.

It became Pidgeon's settled conviction that two choices,

and two choices only, confronted the Presbyterian Church. It could go forward into union and risk substantial losses in eastern Canada. It could draw back and lose the entire west and north. Faced with such alternatives, he did not hesitate in determining his course of action. Schism in the east would be a serious blow to Presbyterianism, he reasoned, but the defection of the entire west would be fatal to its national influence.

Many even today would disagree with this judgment. They would argue that the Presbyterian Church could have stayed out of union and still held many of its members on the frontier. They would argue that even the loss of a region would have been less serious than the disruption of thousands of congregations. It must be remembered, however, that Pidgeon had to make his decision in 1917. Few then foresaw that almost all those who had voted against union would remain out and organize a non-concurring denomination. The precedent most clearly in people's minds was the union of 1875, which had resulted in the formation of the Presbyterian Church of Canada. Before that union there had been considerable opposition in the Kirk, but most had come in immediately, and the rest had followed congregation by congregation. Pidgeon was balancing a risk against what he regarded as a certainty. And even if he had been able to foresee the future, he could never have supported a course of action that would deny to Presbyterianism its national mission.

When he made his decision, it was almost certainly the future of Presbyterianism that was most in his mind. The vision of a united church did not as yet thrill him as it did some of his contemporaries. He was, perhaps, so thoroughly impregnated with Presbyterianism that his imagination did not take hold of the idea. What concerned him was that the Presbyterian Church had to choose between fulfilling itself in union or losing its national character. Only the former course seemed to him worthy.

Important as all these motives undoubtedly were, a much simpler explanation would in large measure account for Pidgeon's actions. By temperament he was a doer. Whenever he was given a responsibility he gave himself to it tirelessly. Is it possible that he became the leader of the church union movement by trying to perform, to the utmost of his ability, his duties as convener of the Board of Home Missions? Certainly his appointment to that office in 1917 was to have incalculable consequences for the future of the Presbyterian Church.

7. Divided on Union

The church union issue precipitated within the Presbyterian Church in Canada the bitterest and most prolonged controversy in Canadian religious history. Even Canadian secular history offers few parallels. The rebellion of 1837 and the conscription dispute of 1917 called forth strong feelings, but in neither case were brothers set so irreconcilably against brothers or colleagues compelled for so long to maintain the formalities of friendship while actively campaigning against one another.

The struggle was made all the more bitter by the inappropriateness of the issue. Those who first suggested union would have been scandalized if they could have foreseen that their proposals would become occasions for further division. The first overtures towards wider union were received with general applause, those with reservations expressing them politely and tentatively. Support for the union was the approved thing.

Once negotiations were under way, it became evident that sentiment among Presbyterians was not unanimously or even overwhelmingly in favour of union. The first overt sign of opposition was John Mackay's speech at the Assembly of 1906. The House of Lords had recently ruled that the Free Church of Scotland could not carry its property into a union, and Mackay warned that Canadian Presbyterians might find their plans wrecked by similar legal difficulties. A plebiscite of members in 1908 showed a substantial minority opposed to union. At the Assembly of 1910, Mackay's impassioned pleas almost carried the day before they were demolished by the debating skill of Principal Patrick.

These setbacks caused less worry than one might suppose. The unionists knew Presbyterianism from within. The Presbyterian way was to discuss proposals thoroughly, even heatedly, and then to accept the decisions of church courts. The unionists knew that the constitution of the Presbyterian Church in Canada contained provisions for changes in doctrine and practice that were absent from the constitution of the supposedly Free Church of Scotland. They regarded the vote of 1908 as a decisive enough verdict in view of the lack of any educational programme preceding it. They expected that the Assembly victory of 1910, soon to be ratified by two-thirds of the presbyteries across the country as required by the Barrier Act, would lead to a decision that would be accepted by all. Even if a few stayed out, as may always happen among Presbyterians, Canadian precedent suggested that they would gradually overcome their scruples. These expectations may seem unreasonable today. They are seen in a better perspective, however, if it is recalled that although many Methodists also voted against the union their entire membership finally entered it.

The turning point for Presbyterianism came when opponents of union began to organize and thereby to commit themselves publicly. After the Assembly of 1912, which postponed consideration of union in the hope of securing eventual unanimity, anti-unionists formed an association to promote the federation of Protestant churches as a substitute for organic union. In 1916, when the Assembly committed the church to union, opponents called a mass rally in St. Andrew's Church, Toronto. Here was organized the Presbyterian Church Association, dedicated no longer to federation but to the preservation of "true-blue" Presbyterianism. By this time Principal D. J. Fraser of Montreal had succeeded to the leadership of the movement, Mackay having resolved in 1912 to go with his church if union were consummated. The opponents of union now constituted a party, united only in their determination to remain separate, but committed unalterably to that. The lines drawn then remain to this day: as early as November 11, 1916, Professor R. E. Welch of Montreal was predicting accurately in a letter to Pidgeon that his college would be among the properties handed over to the non-concurring body.

The truce decreed by the Assembly of 1917 did nothing to resolve the church's inner tensions, the two parties remaining approximately as they had before. In its own way, however, this period of uneasy waiting was decisive for the future of church union. One of the terms of the truce was that congregations should be free to unite locally. Unionists had naturally agreed to this provision, and those against had regarded it as a useful safety valve to lower the pressure for union. The result was such a wave of local unions that by 1921 church union was practically a *fait accompli* in the west and in northern Ontario. Or perhaps it would be more correct to say that Presbyterians in these areas, and many more in parts of old Ontario and the Maritimes, would be hopelessly compromised if the union did not take place.

The union question inevitably arose again in 1921, and the General Assembly determined to press forward as quickly as possible. It reconstituted its union committee, which had been inactive during the truce, and instructed it to take the necessary steps to implement its decision. Anti-unionist representatives were included to ensure that justice would be done to the minority. Pidgeon, who was regarded as a moderate unionist, succeeded Sir Robert Falconer as its convener.

Union committees of the three negotiating churches also sat together as a joint union committee, and under a system of denominational rotation he soon began a year's term as its chairman.

The task as he saw it was that of bringing the new church to birth as expeditiously and as harmoniously as possible, finding ways by which all might come in if that should prove feasible, coming to an amicable arrangement for terms of separation if it should not. The question of union itself he regarded as beyond his terms of reference, for it had been decided by the church long before. He was accordingly not open to suggestions for compromise or delay. Neither did he regard the promotion of union sentiment as the business of his committee—at least not yet. His assignment was simply to devise honourable and effective means of fulfilling his church's commitment to union.

Taking office amid near-unanimous expressions of good will, Pidgeon soon found that as convener of the union committee he was at the centre of a rapidly gathering storm. The end of the truce was the signal for a marshalling of forces, with each side seeking to take up advantageous positions and to discover weaknesses in the other's lines. The military analogy comes naturally, for the Presbyterian Church soon took on the aspect of a battlefield, and many of the champions on both sides were men who had recently returned from war.

During the truce some of the anti-unionists had convinced themselves that the menacing cloud of union would dissipate with the lapse of time. It seemed to them inconceivable that, in view of the size and determination of the declared opposition, the unionists could carry through their plans. Early in 1921, Dr. Ephraim Scott, the editor of the *Presbyterian Record* and one of the most fiery opponents of union, wrote to Pidgeon expressing the hope that the union issue would not be raised again. Pidgeon replied:

I do dread the raising of the Church union question again with all the bitterness and division that it will involve. But I fear it must come. I talked privately with the Western men who brought it up at the Assembly and they were quite emphatic in their statements that it must be settled now and equally emphatic that they in the west were going to unite anyway.

The resurgence of union activity was greeted in the anti-unionist camp with cries of outrage and charges of betrayal. A committee report in 1908 had suggested that without practical unanimity the projected union could not be effective or lasting, and many of the anti-unionists had taken this expression of policy for a promise. With union once more a serious movement, they rushed to perfect their organization. Even some of the unionists had qualms. Principals W. H. Smith of Vancouver and Clarence Mackinnon of Halifax wrote Pidgeon independently on October 5, 1921, to warn against "rushing a split," adding that time would inevitably bring about a growing together.

The situation had changed drastically since 1908, however, and pressures towards union were mounting. Pidgeon's reference to western determination was not mere rhetoric. Principal Edmund H. Oliver of the Presbyterian Theological College in Saskatoon warned him in a letter of June 23, 1921, that if the Assembly had not taken action the local union churches of the west would have precipitated a situation of the utmost seriousness. "As it is, if for a little while the utmost tact and consideration can be employed, the Union movement will not only cease to be a menace here but will be a positive ally." Oliver urged that representatives of the movement should at all costs be brought east to meet the union negotiators, adding that in view of hard times on the prairies it might be necessary to pay the rail fare of leaders like the Honourable W. R. Motherwell. Arrangements were made, and Pidgeon's first meeting as chairman of the joint union committee was also the first meeting at which representatives of the General Council of Local Union Churches were present as corresponding members. These westerners proved to be a trifle bumptious, but the threat of immediate secession was staved off. To the chairman their presence served as a reminder of the calamities that might follow if the church should allow even a suspicion that it was wavering in its resolve.

Despite signs of trouble to come, the first year of Pidgeon's chairmanship was on the whole one of decreasing tension. The minutes of the Presbyterian union committee of May 30, 1921, record Scott's thankfulness for "the spirit of harmony and the unanimity" that had marked the proceedings under Pidgeon's chairmanship. Principal Fraser referred on October 6 to "the sanity and considerateness which characterized the last meetings of the union committee." The Reverend J. S. Shortt, an anti-unionist leader from Alberta, wrote on October 10: "I feel sure that under your chairmanship harmony will prevail, and if we must agree to differ it will not be with feelings other than should prevail among brethren who have so long wrought together in peace and harmony." Pidgeon himself was able to report for his committee in the spring of 1922, "The old bitterness is gone, and must not be allowed to return." In conversation he has recalled that the union committee was made up of reasonable men who were determined to disagree amicably, but correspondents gave him much of the credit. One even suggested that he might qualify for the woe pronounced "when all men speak well of you." He was to be delivered from any danger of that particular woe.

He had his opportunity to escape the coming ordeal. In 1921 he was urged to become the minister of a Presbyterian church in Philadelphia, although he does not seem to have given the call very serious consideration. During the same year he was invited to become Professor of Homiletics at Knox College, Toronto, but he had already decided that the pastorate was to be his life's work.

The Assembly of 1922 took no spectacular action. At the direction of the union committee, R. E. Cassels, K.C., had made a careful study of the assets of the negotiating churches. The anti-unionists objected that they would have to oppose any statement to the Assembly that presupposed union, and they suggested that in view of a serious deficit in mission funds it would be better to have another year of truce before contemplating further action. The committee agreed to present an innocuous report, and contented itself with securing further legal advice on steps necessary to consummate union.

There was to be no truce. It had been possible, perhaps, for anti-unionists to dismiss the resolution of 1921 as merely another in a series that could stretch into an indefinite future. Inventories and lawyer's briefs made the threat concrete and immediate. Within three months the Presbyterian Church Association had organized a series of convocations from coast to coast, and in January, 1923, it secured Dr. J. W. Macnamara as organizing secretary. It was the wish of the unionists, Pidgeon wrote to George A. Brown on April 6, 1923, that the subject should not be raised before the public or even in presbyteries or synods at this stage. In view of anti-unionist activity, however, it had been necessary for the union forces to organize. In October, 1922, a group of unionists meeting in the dining-room of Eaton's in Toronto determined to have one or two key men appointed in each presbytery. George Pidgeon wrote to his brother Leslie on October 19, "The Anti-Unionists have thrown down the gage of battle and unless we start to meet it now, the whole movement will be endangered." He was soon busy raising money and helping to issue literature.

The struggle was now out in the open, but the lines were still shifting. For many Presbyterians, the issues were far from clear; many clung to a dying hope that the deepening chasm might yet be bridged; many ministers remained on the fence, reluctant to commit themselves to a future that was uncertain whichever way they jumped. The year following the Assembly of 1922 was one of the most confused of the whole union era. Friends of union sought means of conciliation, while opponents cast about for alternatives that might yet save the day. Each side hoped that the other would propose an acceptable compromise; each suspiciously examined every proposal from the other camp for hidden implications.

The Lambeth conference of 1920 urged Anglican churches throughout the world to initiate discussions of union. Accordingly, in 1921, the Most Reverend S. P. Matheson, the Primate of the Church of England in Canada, had a committee appointed to meet official representatives of other denominations. The Methodists, whose General Conference met only every four years, were unable to act quickly. They were willing to take part in informal discussions, but the Primate ruled that his committee's terms of reference did not provide for such, and he pressed instead for a separate meeting with the Presbyterian committee. Such a meeting was apparently arranged for the fall of 1921 but did not take place. Pidgeon carried on a lively correspondence with the archbishop throughout the early months of 1922, but after several postponements of the proposed meeting both sides seem to have decided to wait until after the consummation of the immediate union. The highlight of this brief encounter was the publication in May, 1922, of a joint declaration by five Anglican and

five Presbyterian clergymen of Montreal that for the sake of
union they were prepared to accept mutual ordination.

The Primate's initiative put the Presbyterian unionists in
an awkward position. In the best of circumstances it would
have been received with mixed feelings. Including a fourth
party in the negotiations would have involved years of delay
while a new basis of union was being drafted, and ultimate
failure would have compromised much of what had already
been gained. In 1922, with controversy already raging within
the Presbyterian Church, a further complication might have
been fatal to the whole union movement. Pidgeon urged that
his committee had been set up for a particular task and that
wider negotiations should be carried on by another. Throughout the proceedings he insisted on his willingness to confer
and suggested several dates, but he would take no action
without constant consultation with his Methodist and
Congregational colleagues.

There were further complications. Some of the anti-unionists, especially in Montreal, publicly welcomed the Anglican
initiative; several of the signers of the famous declaration were
prominent in their ranks. Described by one unionist as
"aristocrats," they felt more affinity with the Anglicans than
with the Methodists. Untroubled by qualms about disrupting
existing negotiations, they seized the opportunity to complain
that the unionists were evading an opportunity for wider
union. The unionists, on their part, suspected that the Primate
was being influenced by the advice of their opponents. They
were not convinced that his refusal to meet the Methodist
committee was inspired merely by respect for a technicality.
They noted his repeatedly expressed desire not to complicate
existing negotiations, coupled with his repeatedly expressed
readiness to meet the Presbyterian committee separately.
They were particularly disturbed by his omission of any refer-

ence to the Congregationalists, who unlike the Methodists had empowered their committee to deal with the Anglicans. In the strained atmosphere of the time there were natural suspicions of a conspiracy.

Archbishop Matheson was assuredly not trying to scuttle the union by ill-timed intervention. He was following to the letter the instructions of the Lambeth conference. It is quite conceivable, however, that there was contact between him and some of the "high church" Presbyterians within the anti-union party. Many Anglicans sympathized with those Presbyterians who resisted union with the Methodists. They remembered old struggles in which adherents of the established Church of Scotland had stood with them against equalitarian Methodists, and they disliked contemporary Methodists for their ardent espousal of prohibition. Matheson may well have been persuaded by Dr. George Duncan and other anti-unionists that the Presbyterian Church was embarrassed by its involvement with Methodists and Congregationalists, and would welcome an opportunity to seek a more appropriate alliance. Whatever his understanding of the situation, however, his failure to appreciate the impossibility of meeting the Presbyterians outside the context of existing discussions revealed an astonishing lack of perception.

A much more direct threat to the unionist position than the archbishop's diversion was the publication of a pamphlet entitled *Is There Not a Way Out?* by Dr. D. R. Drummond, Secretary of the General Board of the Presbyterian Church in Canada.* Drummond had not previously been identified with either party in the union dispute, although at the Assembly of 1921 he had spoken eloquently of a union in which all the

---

*Dr. Drummond's proposal appeared for the first time in the daily press on April 6, 1923, according to E. L. Morrow, *Church Union in Canada* (Toronto, Allen, 1923), p. 212. The pamphlet, published on April 19, was a revision.

contending parties could find their place. Now, urging the necessity of holding the church together by any honourable means, he proposed a third course that would afford the advantages of union while preventing a Presbyterian schism. The Protestant denominations should federate, combining some of their national enterprises while retaining their separate identities. The union congregations could enter the federation as a separate denomination or in affiliation with existing denominations.

Drummond's bold move could scarcely have been more expertly timed. Many Presbyterians who desired union were now for the first time beginning to realize the price that would have to be paid for it. Anti-unionists were predisposed to any plan that would prevent the fusion of denominations, and they had long been urging greater co-operation as an alternative to organic union. The large number who had no strong feelings for or against union wanted nothing more than a "way out" of the apparent impasse. The anti-unionist party as a whole urged the Drummond proposals as a fair compromise, and some of the leading unionists were claimed as supporters.

Pidgeon was not taken in for a moment. What impressed him immediately was that the projected compromise was but resistance to union under another name. It did not fulfil the commitment to the other negotiating denominations made by the Presbyterian Church in 1916. It could not succeed, for before the union decision could be repealed it would be necessary to perform the impossible feat of persuading two-thirds of the presbyteries to vote it out. Worst of all, in his opinion, it failed to solve the problem posed by the existence of the many union congregations. The plan would set them loose from denominational loyalties. It would perhaps create a new western denomination, and would break faith with those who had entered local unions on the promise that their church would follow them into union. On April 12, 1923, an *ad hoc* committee of unionists from various parts of the church discussed and rejected Drummond's plan as offering no advantages and threatening disaster not only to union but to co-operation.

Despite his misgivings, Pidgeon agreed to take part in a joint meeting on May 23, 1923. There were four unionists, four anti-unionists and four adherents of Drummond's middle way. The meeting achieved nothing. "We were not together five minutes," Pidgeon wrote several other unionists on May 28, "until it became evident that there were only two groups after all, namely, Unionists and those opposed to immediate action. . . . The only remedy that any of the party could see was for the Unionists to quit." He recalls this meeting, at which in the face of a hostile majority he had to warn that no compromise was possible, as one of the most difficult situations of his life.

Whatever its merits, Drummond's proposal came several years too late. The Presbyterian Church had gone too far on the road to union to contemplate turning back, and turning back was all that compromise could mean in 1923. The unionist party held together, although tactically weakened by having been made to appear intransigent. Drummond and his adherents, who were especially strong in Hamilton, showed their colours by merging with the anti-unionist party after the rejection of their suggestion.

Meanwhile, the situation of the church was becoming steadily more desperate. Each party still hoped that time would bring decisive victory, but the immediate prospect was for disruption. Unless the contending forces could agree on the terms of separation, the state would have to step in to determine the many issues affecting property and civil rights that would certainly arise. To Presbyterians, raised in a tradition that jealously guarded "the crown rights of the Redeemer" over against the pretensions of the state, the prospect of such an intervention was intolerable, but the two parties found it impossible to converse with one another.

Both sides were anxious for a viable arrangement. Pidgeon wrote to Judge Swanson of Kamloops on August 23, 1922:

> One thing to which I am giving a good deal of thought and effort is the possibility of getting the moderate unionists and anti-unionists together. I do not see why the two sections of the Church should have to fight one another before the Legislatures and Courts. I believe that there are enough reasonable men on both sides to decide that if we must separate, we shall separate as brothers breaking up a partnership, and go together to the Parliament and Legislatures asking for the things on which both are agreed.

There is good reason to believe that "reasonable men" on the other side were equally desirous of an amicable settlement, but failure to agree on a matter of principle made it impossible to set up an agenda for discussion. Pidgeon recognized that some Presbyterians were conscientiously opposed to union and would not enter it under any conditions. He was willing and even eager to discuss arrangements for the treatment of the non-concurring minority. He would not admit that there could be any discussion of the union itself, which had already been accepted by the church, and he had made up his mind that the chief danger was no longer from the anti-unionists but from "the timid unionist who wants to go still further in conciliatory measures."* The anti-unionists had contended since 1916 that the General Assembly lacked the authority to commit the Presbyterian Church to union; they would therefore discuss terms only on the assumption that the church as such would not enter the union. Presbyterians are notorious for their readiness to subordinate all other considerations to

---

*From a letter to Dr. E. H. Oliver, December 12, 1922.

matters of principle, and disagreement on this one prevented the accommodation desired by both sides.

The crucial issue was the future identity of the Presbyterian Church in Canada. Would it be preserved within The United Church of Canada, or could the non-concurrents claim it for the denomination they intended to set up? In September, 1922, R. E. Knowles publicly raised the issue in the Toronto *Star* by reporting that the two parties had tacitly agreed that those staying out of union would remain in the Presbyterian Church. Pidgeon replied on September 23 that "when a church by proper constitutional procedures unites with other churches, that church as a unit enters the new union," while those that do not enter the union "go out of it to form a new one."

On September 25, Knowles published an interview with D. J. Fraser. The anti-unionist leader was confident that the majority of the Assembly would be too generous to deny the name to the minority. He admitted that Pidgeon's opinion was that of counsel retained by the General Assembly, but added, "This interpretation of the act is a death blow to the proposed union." A lively controversy ensued, with neither side prepared to yield to the other the continuing identity of the Presbyterian Church. To some people today the issue may seem academic, but no one familiar with the history of the Christian church will be surprised that it raised strong feelings. Unhappily failure to agree on it darkened the last years of the union enterprise.

In presenting the report of the union committee to the General Assembly at Port Arthur in 1923, Pidgeon gave most of his attention to the further steps required to consummate the union. The Assembly of 1922 had directed that a bill should be prepared for Parliament and the provincial legislatures, and Pidgeon was prepared for a discussion of its details. Fraser presented a minority report for the anti-unionists on the committee, but this was only for the record. The sensation of the Assembly was an amendment by Drummond resolving that under existing conditions further efforts for organic union would be inadvisable. The anti-unionists supported the amendment, contending that the church had no authority to unite with another. The details of the bill were forgotten, and there ensued a debate in which the merits of the union were discussed with rare eloquence and good temper on both sides. Pidgeon made the final reply for the union committee, urging that "further postponement would expose our church to the charge of expensive and irresolute trifling with problems of vast importance." The Assembly decided by a large majority to enter the union as a church, and to do so "forthwith." This was the final decision of the church as a whole on the matter; the anti-unionists would make no further attempts to reverse it.

Although the most spectacular public phase of the church union controversy was yet to come, it may well be that Pidgeon had already made his most effective contribution to it. During the confusing period from 1921 to 1923, the union cause sometimes seemed to be near collapse. Even today one reads records of the period with a certain disbelief. The Presbyterian Church was on the verge of division, but it still had to operate as a church. Ministers about to part from one another, on an issue that was searing consciences and inflaming passions, had not only to maintain the civilities but to co-operate in raising money, building churches and settling ministers. The Presbyterian Church as they had known it was passing away before their eyes, but the appearance of familiarity and security was still there. It was only natural that even enthusiastic advocates of union would grasp at any proposal for preserving the dissolving image of the known institution, even if they half suspected the flaw in the proposal. It has been suggested that Pidgeon's firmness saved the union in this interlude of uncertainty. The claim may be exaggerated for, as he himself saw clearly, any attempt to reverse the church's decision would have had grave and incalculable consequences. Nevertheless, there can be little doubt that it was his leadership that preserved the morale of the unionist party and kept its sense of purpose intact.

Pidgeon's great strength as a leader during this period was his refusal to be diverted from the main issue. He was as sensitive as any other to the bitterness of impending separation, and more aware than most of the price that would have to be paid for union. He was still a disciple of MacVicar, however, dedicated to the proposition that a duty seen ought to be a duty performed. He was applying to the church union controversy the same dogged determination that had carried him through many struggles over moral issues. And always, as he faced the prospect of schism in the east, he had one ear cocked for the impatient voice with which the west insisted that it would unite even at the cost of secession. For George Pidgeon the issue was always simple: Presbyterianism could maintain its honour and its national stature only by fulfilling its commitment to union.

8. Church Union Achieved

After the Port Arthur Assembly of 1923 the union struggle entered its final and most disruptive stage. The issue was no longer whether the union should take place but what proportion of its human and material resources the church should take with it into The United Church of Canada. From 1923 to 1925, Presbyterians fought a civil war on two fronts. At Ottawa and the provincial capitals, rival delegations sponsored and opposed legislation that would recognize the union and give effect to its provisions affecting property rights. In congregations throughout the country, supporters and opponents of union sought the votes of individual church members.

There was no dialogue between the two contenders, no possibility of a mutually acceptable compromise, no agreement to wash dirty linen in private. Even after the Assembly a few last-ditch attempts were made to establish contact, but they were doomed to failure. Dr. R. W. Dickie of Montreal, who dreaded disruption almost as much as he disliked the prospect of union, suggested to Pidgeon that Presbyterian congregations should be allowed to maintain their identity and their doctrinal standards within a united church. The anti-unionist executive quickly disowned the plan. At the request of the union committee, Pidgeon made another effort on October 1 to persuade the anti-unionist leaders to confer on terms of separation. Fraser replied favourably on October 4, but added that since legal details were chiefly involved it would be appropriate to carry on further discussion through attorneys.

Further correspondence drew from the counsel for the minority the reply that negotiation would be useless unless it was first admitted that the Presbyterian Church could not enter union as a church.

A final break came on January 25, 1924, when the opponents of union applied to the Supreme Court of Ontario for a writ of injunction prohibiting Pidgeon and other members of his committee from proceeding further with the union. The case was never taken to court, and the minority made no further direct attempts to stop the union. The application had the effect, however, of putting on public record its opposition to a statement in the Basis of Union that "God in the gospel freely offers His all-sufficient salvation to all men." Although angered by this attempt to invoke the civil power in an ecclesiastical dispute, the unionists valued the writ so highly as propaganda for their cause that they had a thousand copies printed and distributed without comment.

The incident of the writ, fantastic as it must seem to a generation accustomed to interdenominational good will, is typical of the last two years of the church union struggle. From lofty discussions of principle at the Assembly, the contestants quickly turned to the rough-and-ready infighting of the hustings. Canadian election campaigns at that time were marked by breaches of taste and lapses from truth that would be unacceptable today. Christian ministers outdid the politicians in vituperation, and the struggle took on an added virulence because there was no possibility of a return engagement in four or five years. Most protagonists on both sides were men of honour and integrity. Anyone with a talent for demagogy or intrigue had ample opportunity, however, and with feelings inflamed even honest men found it easy to justify knavery. Campaign headquarters had to maintain a constant lookout for absurd but plausible slanders, such as a rumour that Canadians would be taxed for the support of the new "national" church. Even the cleaner aspects of the campaign required pamphlets and canvasses, lobbying and public debate.

For Pidgeon the new situation meant a more public and more controversial role. Hitherto he had felt that as chairman of the union committee he should be an impartial administrator of the church's policy rather than the spokesman of a party. As late as August, 1922, he reported that his committee wanted him to be strictly impartial, and most of the opponents of union respected his attempt to appear so, at least in public. In fact he was most averse to public controversy over church union and found it difficult to be patient with those who provoked it. His attitude was that the church's decision ought to be accepted by all who could conscientiously do so, and that those who could not accept it should withdraw gracefully without trying to involve others in schism. This was, in the circumstances, an unrealistic hope, based on a premise that the anti-unionists did not accept, but undoubtedly it delayed the launching of a vigorous unionist effort to reach the public.

By the fall of 1922, Pidgeon recognized that the Presbyterian Church was not going to be spared the public ordeal he dreaded. During the next year, therefore, he was active in rallying the unionist forces and in obtaining financial support. His own intense public campaigning began only after Port Arthur, however, when the church determined to "proceed forthwith" to union. The union committee decided in July to set up a Joint Central Bureau of Literature and Information. Pidgeon was a member of the committee appointed to direct it, and he wrote several pamphlets supporting union. That fall he began to address public meetings, and from this point on his home became a centre of unionist strategy.

With public involvement came public criticism. Personal feelings were not spared in the controversy, and Pidgeon's central position naturally attracted abuse. One canard had it that he was to be "pope" of the United Church at a salary of $15,000–later $30,000–per year. He never replied in kind. His character was indeed so irreproachable that most innuendoes were self-defeating, although he would remain to many "the man who took our church away from us."

The immediate problem for the unionists was to secure legislation. This was considered necessary for several reasons. The Presbyterian Church in Canada was not incorporated, but the Methodist Church was, and so were several of the Presbyterian boards. Legislation was not needed to bring about union, but counsel agreed from the beginning that without it the disposal of trusts and properties would give rise to endless complications. A further consideration was that the framers of the Basis of Union wanted to ensure that the united church would have control of its own doctrine and undeniable authority to enter further unions. They remembered the difficulties raised in Scotland at the time of the Free Church union, and although they were confident that the Presbyterian Church in Canada was legally competent to unite, they wanted to make doubly sure. Besides, legislation was needed to give the Methodist Church power to alter its doctrinal standards; if controversy had arisen in *that* church, union might have been impossible.

Apart from the opposition within the Presbyterian Church, the securing of legislation would have been a mere formality. In the absence of agreement between the two parties, it had to be fought for in legislatures and committees consisting of members of all religious denominations. Canada's federal system posed a further problem. Incorporation required a national act, but since the provinces control matters of property, bills had to be passed in each legislature. For two years, therefore, politicians from coast to coast became arbiters of Presbyterian law and doctrine. Technically the issue was kept independent of party lines, but it was impossible to prevent politicians from reckoning practical advantages to themselves, their parties or their denominations.

Without legislation the Presbyterian Church would theoretically have taken its entire property into the union with it. As early as 1914, however, the church had decided that congregations should have the right to stay out and that the act of incorporation of the united church should "make proper provision to guard the rights and privileges" of the minority. In 1922 the lawyers retained by the union committee advised that legislation would almost certainly fail unless there was "fair and generous treatment" for the minority. Such treatment had been customary in earlier Presbyterian unions, and there was no disposition to refuse it now. The church proposed not only that non-concurring congregations should be allowed to retain their property but that, contrary to precedent, the assets of the denomination as a whole should be divided. Despite this generosity, there was room for haggling between the parties over the details of the division.

Until the very end, the anti-unionist leaders had some hopes of blocking the union altogether. They knew that they could not command a majority in their own assembly, but they hoped to persuade legislators either that union was not within the church's competence or that Presbyterians as a whole needed to be saved from the tyranny of their leaders. Some of them may even have supposed that if legislation were denied, the unionists would give up their project; if so, they would have been disappointed, for Pidgeon and other leaders were determined to let all the property go if necessary. The more realistic strategists among the anti-unionists sought a rewording of the legislation that would allow the unionists to found a new church if they wished while retaining for themselves the continuing identity of the Presbyterian Church—so far, that is, as legislation could affect such a matter.

The circumstances made for extreme bitterness, and behind the bitterness was the old contentious question of the church's right to enter union as a church. The unionists took their stand on the church's spiritual freedom, arguing that the state had no right to deny the expressed desire of the three churches to unite or to interfere in the spiritual arrangements for union. The anti-unionists complained of coercion, largely on the ground that congregations would automatically become part of the united church unless they voted themselves out of it. They also complained that no general vote of the membership had been taken for many years, but did not ask for one and declined to be bound even if one were held. Behind the scenes there was some negotiation on points of detail, but neither side would yield on the main issue.

Although the leaders on both sides were mainly concerned with matters of principle, legislative committees spent most of their time discussing marginal issues. Of these the division of common property and the manner of taking congregational votes proved to be the most contentious, and there were times when a committee would spend hours over a point of detail and then decide by a snap vote an issue of vital importance to both sides. Lobbyists needed to be patient and above all vigilant.

The ablest political representative of the unionist side was unquestionably Leslie Pidgeon, then minister of Augustine Church, Winnipeg. During 1924 he prepared the unionist argument for presentation, met individual parliamentarians at Ottawa, and piloted the bill through the Private Bills Committee and the House of Commons. When time was available, he also met legislative committees in the Maritimes and the west. His grasp of legal detail was invaluable to his cause, and, although he antagonized some by the sharpness of his logic, he proved his ability to speak to legislators in language they could understand. It is difficult to imagine how the bill could have passed without his assistance.

George Pidgeon spent most of his time in Toronto, attending to his pastoral duties, directing the central committee and watching proceedings in the Ontario legislature. Of all the provinces, Ontario was the one that caused most concern to the unionist leaders. There anti-union sentiment was strongest. There, too, the strongest memories of old interdenominational tensions persisted. The situation was further complicated by an imminent plebiscite on prohibition, and some "wet" supporters were eager to punish the Methodists for their leadership in the crusade against alcohol. Another serious cause of anxiety was the reluctance of moneyed men to support the union cause.

Anticipating a hard struggle, George Pidgeon sent out letters to unionists in every provincial riding on January 25, 1924, urging them to find key men who could approach members of the legislature. Many replies told of serious difficulties. At the legislative committee, affairs went badly. Anglican and Roman Catholic MPP's lined up almost solidly against the unionist bill. The committee adopted an amendment that would have created a new united church while leaving the present Presbyterian, Methodist and Congregational bodies in existence. The effect was not only to admit the contention of the non-unionist Presbyterians that they represented the continuing Presbyterian Church in Canada, but to grant a similar status to a negligible Congregational minority that had made no such claim and to a Methodist minority that did not even exist. To the unionists this action represented an intolerable invasion by the state of the rights of the church, and in desperation they temporarily withdrew the bill.

Leslie Pidgeon, hearing the news in Ottawa, was thunderstruck. On April 8, he dispatched to his brother the only angry letter on record between them:

To say that I believe you have made a mistake is not to begin to say what I feel. I cannot agree that you will be better off by withdrawing it. It means defeat, and I believe it will mean defeat here and in the Maritimes.

George replied on the tenth that he had wanted to go ahead but that the committee had decided otherwise. The wets and the Anglicans had been unanimous in opposition, and with the prospect of an impossible bill no course but withdrawal seemed open. He added that he was far from satisfied with the state of the unionist organization in Toronto. The movement operated through a battery of committees, each expecting to be consulted before action was taken. The resulting delays could be very expensive. The Methodists, over-anxious to avoid embarrassing their Presbyterian allies, were withholding support. On April 14, George Pidgeon wrote jubilantly to his brother that he had at last succeeded in getting through a unity of command, with Sir James Wood as chairman of a central committee. It was too late, however, to do anything that year in Ontario.

The union fared scarcely better in the Private Bills Committee of the House of Commons. Leslie Pidgeon presented his most persuasive arguments. The unionists provided an impressive array of ministerial talent. A few weeks earlier, George had written his brother that he intended to let others do the talking at Ottawa. Leslie had replied on March 22, "History is being made. You must be here both seeing and hearing, and being seen and heard." Now he was in Ottawa to make the final reply for the union side.

At this time the anti-unionists, claiming that most members of the Presbyterian Church were on their side, were arguing that the voice of the people should prevail over the constitutional decisions of church courts. Pidgeon's usual style in debate was deliberate and serious, but in his statement to the committee he responded to this claim with a rare burst of sarcasm. "Is not this whole argument directed against Presbyterianism as a system? . . . If the system is so rotten, why are they fighting so hard to maintain it?"*

On this occasion Dr. Ephraim Scott, formerly a personal friend, refused George Pidgeon's proffered hand. "I have no improper feeling towards you," he wrote. "But when you were there for the express purpose of trying to do me so great a wrong, attempting to drive me by civil law against my conviction of right; then it was not *honest for you to offer your hand or for me to take it.*"† As yet, however, Scott had little of which to complain. Although the Private Bills Committee seemed sympathetic to the unionist case, a mass accession of French-Canadian members at the last minute carried an amendment to delay the union for two years and to refer to a civil court the power of the General Assembly to consummate it.

This was the ebb of the tide. New Brunswick had meanwhile passed enabling legislation, and prospects in several other provinces were good. At Ottawa the unionists led by Leslie Pidgeon worked harder than ever. T. W. Bird, a Presbyterian minister and Progressive MP, thus described the result:

It was amazing to see DD's and prospective Moderators manipulating the elements of a complex situation in the approved manner, with original touches of their own. We owe much to the other members of the Law and Legislation Committee who did a rare thing on Parliament Hill: they revived a Private Bill that had been killed in committee.‡

---

*Stenographic report of the presentation to the Private Bills Committee of The United Church of Canada Act, in the United Church Archives, pp. 790, 791.
†Italics Scott's. The letter, dated May 28, 1924, was sent only on July 8.
‡*The United Church Observer*, Vol. XII, No. 7 (June 1, 1950), p. 9.

The final passage was far from easy. Mackenzie King, the Prime Minister, was hostile to the bill, and amendments would have referred the bill to the courts and even changed the name of the united church. Support came from Arthur Meighen, the Leader of the Opposition, and the Progressive group was unanimously behind the unionists. The bill was passed eventually on July 19. The Ontario legislature passed its own bill in 1925, omitting the provisions that had been unacceptable in 1924, but compelling congregations that did not enter union to join the denomination that would be founded by the non-concurrents. The anti-unionists agreed in the end not to oppose the bill on condition that Knox College should be awarded to them. The entire faculty and most of the student body were in favour of union, and Principal Alfred Gandier was one of its most militant supporters. Nevertheless the college authorities agreed to give up a fine new building for the sake of a settlement.

While legal issues were being determined in legislative corridors, the opposing forces were already actively lining up support among the Presbyterian membership. The church as a whole had made up its mind to unite, but individual congregations were free to remain out if a majority of members so decided. If the legal aspects of the union struggle encouraged parliamentary intrigue, the necessity of lining up local support invited public agitation and private innuendo. Although in times of affluence congregations seem to replace their buildings with little reluctance, they become strangely attached to them in times of stress. Where a few votes might determine the disposition of congregational property, there was a powerful temptation to get them by fair means or foul, and men of local influence did not always feel the sense of responsibility that normally restrained denominational leaders.

The anti-unionists were under special pressure to disturb

the peace. Since, by the terms of the Act, congregations not voting would become part of the united church, it often required the initiative of the anti-unionists to force a vote. Their party naturally attracted a fanatical fringe of diehards who were prepared to hurl at the unionists any charge that came readily to hand. Unionists were aggrieved that responsible anti-unionists did nothing to repudiate such ambiguous support. George Pidgeon was especially shocked that known modernists like Principal Fraser and Professor Thomas Eakins of the Presbyterian College at Montreal should allow their party in its campaign literature to accuse unionists of heresy, and in March of 1925 he sought affidavits from students testifying to theological statements by the two teachers. One sympathizes with his feelings, while appreciating the desperation in a time of stress of a group that had to stir up public controversy or fail by default.

As the campaign proceeded, it became clear not only that many congregations would remain out of union but that congregations everywhere would be split. As late as January, 1924, Pidgeon was in the name of the union committee advising congregations to enter or remain out of union as units.* He was soon to change his stand. When the anti-unionists declared their intention of invading every congregation to force a vote, he decided that the united church could not afford to lose the strength of unionist minorities in non-concurring congregations. Still mindful of the west and north, he felt the need of a solid eastern base of financial support and ministerial supply. For no decision did the church union committee receive so much adverse criticism. In any case, however, the issue was settled by forces beyond the control of any of the participants. Congregations were so

---

*Letter to M. B. Davidson, January 4, 1924. "Whichever way the vote goes, let all go and do not rend the individual church asunder."

thoroughly rent by controversy that remaining together would have been unthinkable.

Voting in individual congregations began on December 10, 1924. In the Maritimes and in the west, most churches decided for union by large majorities, although a few congregations that had previously made local union arrangements were so stirred by the appeal to denominational loyalty that they voted themselves out. In Ontario, always the centre of anti-unionist activity, the results were a severe shock to Pidgeon. As many large congregations registered adverse votes, he consoled himself with the strength of unionist minorities, but his earlier hope that all but irreconcilables might come in was proving vain. Bloor Street Church gave a large majority for union, although a few of its most prominent families were strongly in the other camp.

Early 1925 was a season of widespread dislocation. The church officially advised congregations to hold together until the inception of union, but in many cases the contending parties could not separate quickly enough. In some places, minorities were being left without buildings or without pastors; in others, outlying congregations were sundered from their parent churches. Most difficult of all was the situation of ministers, mostly union supporters, who lost their congregations in the vote. Many of these were not active partisans but cautious men who had tried to avoid committing themselves in order to maintain peace in their congregations, only to find in the end that an active anti-union canvass had taken place without their knowledge. Ministers and congregations turned in their time of trouble to the chairman of the church union committee; it is obvious from correspondence that some held him personally responsible for their difficulties and expected him to extricate them. Pidgeon responded in his usual activist way, giving advice freely and writing many

letters on behalf of ministers left out of work. Much of his
time in these months must have been given to the details
of reconstruction.

At the last General Assembly of the Presbyterian Church
in Canada, convening on June 3, 1925, George Pidgeon was
elected moderator. On June 10, the church became part of
The United Church of Canada. Despite setbacks, it carried
more than seventy per cent of its membership into the union.

In telling the story of the union controversy almost
exclusively in terms of George Pidgeon's relation to it, I have
doubtless unwittingly done less than justice to some of the
other participants. From 1921 to 1923 his role overshadowed
that of any other on the Presbyterian side. In the later stage
several others became almost equally prominent. R. J. Wilson
was in charge of publicity and literature. John W. Woodside,
a late convert, supervised the vote-taking. Leslie Pidgeon
peregrinated from capital to capital. Gershom W. Mason and
others attended to vital legal details. Unlike several of the
others, George Pidgeon remained the full-time pastor of his
own congregation. It would be difficult, however, to over-
estimate his importance to the union cause.

In the first place, his position within Presbyterianism
naturally drew attention to him. He was a veteran of moral
crusades and an expert on the problems of the home mission
field. In a controversy in which theological professors were
prominent on both sides, it counted that he was the pastor
of a large and stategic congregation in Toronto. We was a
preacher of increasing reputation, respected for his evangelical
soundness even by those who feared change, and his Sunday
School column had given him a wide circle of readers and
correspondents. As chairman of the union committee, he was
the natural spokesman for the unionist position. Newspapers
turned to him for statements on the issue and featured his

public addresses, and the attacks that inevitably followed only increased his prominence.

He was also the strategist who co-ordinated the entire effort. By nature he was a planner who kept the intended goal in view and refused to be distracted by the details in the foreground. A minister who had been his assistant at Bloor Street recalls that he never went into a meeting without having determined in advance what he hoped to achieve; he was ready to accept suggestions, but he was never unprepared. He was able to do this because he could readily turn his mind from the immediate question and regain his perspective on it. This quality served him well in a period of turmoil and uncertainty. He was a centre of calm in a whirlwind of hysteria.

The church union movement owed much to Pidgeon's good conscience in the matter. As the divisiveness of the issue became apparent, many unionists were paralyzed by doubts, and some found themselves in the astonishing position of remaining out of a union they favoured in order to avoid a split they were only aggravating. Pidgeon never wavered in his assurance that his cause was right. Undoubtedly a streak of stubbornness helped him to stay on the course he had set for himself. Behind this stubbornness, however, was not mere prejudice but a lifelong habit of formulating a plan of action and then sticking to it.

Of all the assets that George Pidgeon brought to the leadership of the unionist cause, the greatest were qualities of character. Even in the bitterest days of controversy, few suspected his motives or doubted his integrity. And even beyond integrity he showed forth a quality of sanctity that disarmed criticism. "There's no fighting the Pidgeons," went a common saying. "Leslie is too clever, and George is too good." The saw took too little account of George's cleverness or Leslie's goodness, but there was truth in the caricature. The church union movement gained from the leadership of a man of prayer who meditated on the Bible, preached it and lived it. Especially notable was his refusal to be drawn into the battle of invective then raging, although he had his private opinions of some of his opponents. He gave dignity to what threatened to become merely a sordid brawl.

Alongside his holiness of life must be set his reforming zeal. He was not only spiritual but spirited. Despite his service at the front with the YMCA, it is difficult to imagine Pidgeon as a man of war. In peacetime campaigns, however, he was an inspiring leader who maintained the morale of his forces. He had demonstrated this quality in the days of moral reform, and one suspects that despite the insults he could enjoy a good contest. He detested schism and shrank from a break with Presbyterian colleagues, but when anti-union firebrands were about to invade Winnipeg, he could advise his brother to "show them no mercy." George Pidgeon was a fighting saint of unity, and the sanctity and the fighting spirit combined to rally his supporters.

Unfortunately the controversy did not turn out exactly as he would have liked, and some have held him responsible for the split that ensued. This had become inevitable, although some failed to see it, long before he was given the direction of the church union committee. He saw this at the end, if perhaps not at the beginning. Although he must have had moments of bitter disappointment, he was never oppressed by regrets. If he had one regret, indeed, it was that he had not fought harder and sooner, but he was willing to sacrifice much for the satisfaction of knowing that throughout the struggle he had been scrupulously fair to his opponents.

9. Representative United Churchman

Those who planned services marking the inception of The United Church of Canada on June 10, 1925, reserved major roles for the executive heads of the three uniting denominations. George Pidgeon, as Presbyterian moderator, took charge of a meeting in Massey Hall in the afternoon. Along with the others, as well as the moderator of the General Council of Local Union Churches, he declared the formal adherence of his church at the inaugural service in the Mutual Street Arena. Then he presided at the first celebration of Holy Communion within the United Church.

The order of service followed on this occasion was the one he had long used at Bloor Street. The bread and wine were distributed in Presbyterian fashion to communicants seated in the pews, and all were asked to hold them so that they might partake of each simultaneously. This latter custom was unfamiliar to most of the visitors, having been made possible only by the recent introduction of individual communion cups. So impressive was the service that this practice has become general within the United Church, superseding even among most former Methodists the custom of going forward to partake at a communion rail. Recent liturgical trends have been in a somewhat different direction, but it is no exaggeration to say that Pidgeon's usage has been a dominant influence upon the worship of the first United Church generation.

Although it was intended that the first moderator should be elected by ballot without nominations, the general expectation was that Dr. S. D. Chown would receive most of the votes. He seemed the obvious choice. As general superintendent of the Methodist Church, he had given leadership to the union movement for many years, and he had been able to bring his entire denomination into the union. Moreover, he held a position in his own communion that was without parallel in either of the others. The Methodist general superintendency was a permanent office. Inherited from the earlier Methodist Episcopal Church, it lacked the spiritual prerogatives of the Anglican episcopate, but it wielded far more power than any single bishop could command. A Presbyterian moderator, elected for a one-year term, was a mere figurehead in comparison.

When the moment of the election came, Chown astounded the commissioners by declining to stand. He gave as one reason the fact that he was over seventy, but added that in the circumstances he believed that it would be better to elect a former Presbyterian. The renunciation made, the council acted without hesitation. Chown moved that a ballot be cast for George Pidgeon, and he was elected unanimously. Chown's gesture was magnificently generous, as Pidgeon gratefully recognized. Chown was entitled to the honour, and his age precluded its being offered to him again. The gesture was also magnificently wise. Chown had made his contribution to the union and would soon pass off the stage. Pidgeon's election assured the exhausted Presbyterian group that it would not be engulfed in a Methodist majority, and it gave the United Church a leader who would help to guide it for many years.

Granted five months' leave by his congregation, Pidgeon set off immediately to do some ecclesiastical fence-mending abroad. Long before union, leaders had recognized the importance of securing the good will of denominational colleagues in other countries. Most major communions were linked together in international organizations, and the claim of The United Church of Canada to represent the continuing life of its constituent denominations would command considerably more respect if backed by their recognition. To some of their leaders, however, wider union seemed audacious and possibly fraught with danger to the integrity of the faith.

During 1923 and 1924, Pidgeon had corresponded with several Scottish churchmen, winning considerable sympathy for his case although drawing the tactful suggestion that The United Church of Canada might most appropriately start a new federation in conjunction with a proposed united church in Australia. In 1924, Dr. Clarence Mackinnon and Dr. C. W. Gordon (Ralph Connor) made such a favourable impression in Britain that recognition by the Presbyterian Alliance seemed assured. Pidgeon had been appointed as one of those who should press the case of the United Church at the meeting of the Council of the Alliance at Cardiff, Wales, in 1925. He had even accepted an invitation to preach in Cardiff that would have required him to leave Canada on June 17, cancelling the engagement only when he was persuaded that his presence at the General Council would be essential.

Pidgeon left for Wales with the authority of the moderatorship. He and his colleagues were successful in their mission: both sections of the Alliance eventually accepted the standing of The United Church of Canada and received the non-concurrent Presbyterian Church as a new member. From Cardiff he proceeded to Edinburgh, where he preached on I Corinthians 13 to Kirkmen and spoke on church union to a congregation of the United Free Church of Scotland. He was able to assure conservative Scottish leaders that the United Church was sound, and especially that union with Methodists would not mean a loss of churchmanship. In August he accompanied Chancellor R. P. Bowles of Victoria University to the

Wesleyan Methodist Conference at Lincoln. Dr. James
Endicott and Dr. T. Albert Moore, along with Dr. Mackinnon,
would later make a more formal—and a successful—approach
to the Oecumenical Methodist Conference.

Back in Canada, then turbulent with industrial strife,
Pidgeon set a precedent for future moderators by travelling
extensively. In September he attended the first Maritime Conference, visiting most of the towns of the area en route. Here
someone referred to him as "the apostle of winsomeness." The
title has a quaint sound today, but coming only a few months
after the end of the union controversy it was a remarkable
tribute to his good temper. By January he had visited ten of
eleven conferences, and in the spring he travelled to New-
foundland. He spoke to a pastor's convention in Ohio and
preached to a gathering of churchmen in Toledo. Meanwhile
the prohibition issue had been raised in Ontario again, and
he found time to campaign for a favourite cause.

In September the General Council sent out a message,
obviously drafted by the moderator, summoning church members "to intercede for what our fathers called a revival of
religion." In January he sent out a letter to the church encouraging special services and prayer groups during the weeks
before Easter, with special emphasis on education in the
doctrine of The United Church of Canada. Such moderatorial
encyclicals could easily become matters of routine, and indeed
they were to be somewhat discredited in the future by too
frequent association with financial appeals. Pidgeon's messages
were never motivated by a mere readiness to do what was
expected of him. He was intensely anxious that the union
should be not a merger of resources but a spiritual adventure,
and he was never happier than when he was organizing a
campaign, planning rallies and stirring up "what our fathers
called a revival of religion."

The honour of the moderatorship was speedily followed by others. In April, 1926, Victoria University made him an honorary Doctor of Divinity, and Yale bestowed a similar degree in June. Some suggested that Pidgeon should be elected for a second term. The tenure of moderators of the United Church was set at two years, but the first moderator had been elected for only one. There may have been some feeling that he had not received his full measure of time, but if so nothing came of it and Dr. James Endicott was elected in 1926. It is customary for former moderators to act as deputies to their successors, however, and Pidgeon had many opportunities to represent his church. One was at the union in 1929 bringing together almost all the branches of Scottish Presbyterianism under the name of the original Church of Scotland, where he headed the United Church delegation. Even apart from such formal occasions, his role in the last years of the union movement, and his unique position as first moderator, led many to regard him more than any other as the United Church's representative before the world.

From the outset Pidgeon regarded the union as a success surpassing expectations. "As I visited the newly-united Churches from Coast to Coast," he wrote in his moderatorial message, "I was impressed with the sheer joy with which they came together." Many years later he recalled the richness each group had discovered in sharing the others' traditions of worship and corporate life, and his enthusiasm for union only increased with the passing of time. Nevertheless, he was troubled by the failure of the union to give an immediate impetus to the revival for which he longed. His concern was already evident in the call of General Council in 1925:

We are encamped on the borders of our promised land; if we go forward in response to the divine command, immediate conquest is assured; if we fail, the forty years of wandering in the desert will be too brief to prepare our children to gain back the ground that we shall have lost.

By January 11, 1928, he was writing to Clarence Mackinnon, "There seems to be a sense of spiritual need through the Church deeper than anything I have ever seen." He urged that the next General Council "should certainly inaugurate a movement toward a deep spiritual life and real action in winning men to Christ." This concern was to determine the pattern of Pidgeon's ministry over the next decade.

His uneasiness reflected a mood of discouragement widely prevalent within the church. The first years of union were difficult and in some ways disappointing. Inevitably there was a painful period of readjustment. Ministers and congregations of diverse backgrounds had to be fitted together as a working denomination, and the broken Presbyterian congregations constituted a particular problem. Many lost buildings had to be replaced; many newly united congregations required expanded facilities. People who for years had devoted their energies to advocating an ideal now had to find the money to pay for it, and some of the more passive supporters had probably reckoned that the economies of union would enable them to pay less than they had paid before. A scarcity of well-defined rules and precedents further hampered the church in working out its problems, and the time of church courts was apt to be frittered away in the arguments of amateur ecclesiastical lawyers.

The union was particularly unfortunate in its timing. Conceived in a period of unusual growth and evangelistic activity, the United Church came to birth when the vitality of Christian faith was declining throughout the western world, when many people were turning away from the church and its traditional scale of values. Most of the troubles of the time could not fairly be blamed on the union or even traced to specifically Canadian sources. They inevitably affected the morale of the United Church, however, and the theological trends of the

period seemed to give point to earlier anti-unionist charges
that the new church would be creedless and atomistic. Yet
there were few hints of nostalgia for the old order, although a
discontented fraction of the Methodists may have found a
more congenial atmosphere in some of the newer sects.

It was natural that during the period of growing together
Pidgeon should constantly be called upon for advice, and the
calls extended far beyond his term as moderator. Requests for
rulings on points of church law he resisted as well as he could,
pleading that he had no authority to make them, but some
urgent situations involved him in lengthy correspondence.
Requests for personal advice and help he dealt with
generously, and the records of some filled bulging files. A
friend has suggested that Pidgeon was liberal beyond the
limits of prudence with personal recommendations. The fault,
if any, was due not to heedlessness but to an almost reckless
faith in the potentialities of human nature.

A large segment of his correspondence during this period
dealt with the hardships of displaced ministers. One of the
inevitable and intended results of church union was to effect
local amalgamations that would free ministers for service elsewhere, but several factors made it difficult to make the necessary personal adjustments in an orderly way. Local congregations were left free to unite or not as they wished, and so many
amalgamations had already taken place in small communities
that it was commonly thought the process could not go much
further. Instead, there was another wave of local unions. Many
small neighbourhood churches in cities came together, and a
large number of Presbyterian minority groups adhered to
nearby Methodist churches rather than start small new congregations. Presbyterian ministers came into union in larger
proportion than their flocks, so that the absorption of many
minority groups placed them under a double handicap.

The church had to pay a heavy price for its temporary ministerial surplus. Inevitably there was a certain amount of recrimination. Presbyterians who had lost all for the sake of union felt that they should be provided for, if not necessarily rewarded. Often the only answer could be to arrange for an appointment to a predominantly Methodist pastorate, and then former Methodists took fright. Presbyterians envied Methodists their finesse with settlement committees, while Methodists resented the Presbyterian knack of impressing a congregation with a single sermon. Buried in Pidgeon's files are many letters of complaint from displaced Presbyterians and of counter-complaint from replaced Methodists, some written at white heat.

Ministers who had appointments feared to give them up. Some outstayed their welcome, while others escaped by arranging pastoral exchanges with ministers of similar income. Conference settlement committees followed an exchange system of their own, allowing one minister in only when they were sure that another was leaving. A real-life game of musical chairs always left some ministers out of its ever-narrowing circle. The results were deplorable. Congregations and ministers alike suffered in morale from deadlocks that no one dared to break, and the church as a whole was hindered from thinking in national terms.

Most serious of all was the inevitable loss of vigorous young men. Theological graduates almost had to apologize for seeking pastorates. Those who could afford it undertook postgraduate study, thereby postponing the inevitable day of looking for placement. Many of these found pastorates in the United States, while others founded a tradition of Canadian scholarship in American theological seminaries. The number of recruits fell, foreshadowing a day when the ministry would age and an acute shortage would develop.

If the Canadian experience of union teaches a single unquestionable lesson, it is that promoters of a future plan should provide some means of instituting a national policy of ministerial settlement for at least the first few years. The United Church of Canada had no such machinery. Congregations gave priority to their own needs, conferences looked after their own men, and officials at headquarters were blamed for a situation about which they could do little. Special cases of hardship could be met only by appealing to men of influence.

Pidgeon received more than his share of such appeals, and he gave them a great deal of his time. He felt with special keenness the plight of former Presbyterian ministers whose congregations had rejected their advice to enter union, and he wrote many letters on their behalf. With balanced judgment, however, he refused to let personal sympathy override broader considerations of policy. He was anxious both that congregations should be served by suitable men and that ministers with something to say should be placed where they could be heard, and in fitting the man to the congregation he paid little attention to the complaints of conferences seeking to balance incoming with outcoming pastors. He was particularly eager to retain for the United Church some of the brilliant younger men who could help to shape its future, and only with the greatest reluctance advised some of them to seek positions temporarily in the United States. One senses throughout the correspondence his continuing concern that the church should not lose sight of its national mission.

While making its own internal readjustments, the United Church had to deal with unfinished business arising out of the Presbyterian split. As the last General Assembly of the Presbyterian Church in Canada was dissolving into union to the strains of the *Hallelujah Chorus,* the non-concurring group withdrew to carry on what it claimed to be the same General

Assembly. Here then were two denominations, each claiming to be the Presbyterian Church in Canada and thereby denying the title to the other. Bitterness was inevitable, but inevitably also the two would have to find some basis of coexisting and even of co-operating. For this task of reconciliation Pidgeon felt a special responsibility, although his strong opinions about the principle in dispute made it impossible for him simply to ignore past quarrels.

For several years relations with Presbyterian churches in Britain continued to give concern. G. Campbell Wadsworth, then a student at Edinburgh, wrote to Pidgeon that members of the high church party in the Scottish Kirk were looking askance at the union but that he was doing his best to reassure them. British friends reported that emissaries of the non-concurrents were actively enlisting sympathy for their cause and encouraging ministers to fill the gaps in their ranks. The anti-unionist position was being set forth in publications not only in Britain and the United States but even on the continent, and suitable replies had to be framed. Trouble arose even over prospective Presbyterian immigrants from Britain, who were apparently being told that there was only one Presbyterian church in Canada. The situation was particularly acute in Ireland. Ministers of recent Irish origin had been prominent in the anti-union party in Canada, and there was a good deal of sympathy for them at home. A list of Irishmen in the United Church ministry was duly assembled, and the Presbyterian Church of Ireland eventually gave equal recognition to both Canadian bodies. Continuous cultivation of the Presbyterian Alliance was also felt to be necessary, and Pidgeon was appointed a representative in 1925.

Moderate men in both churches regretted the continuance of controversy into the period of reconstruction, but in view of the international nature of Presbyterianism there seemed to be no way of keeping the quarrel at home. Pending a new equilibrium, leaders on both sides were kept on the alert. For the United Church, probably no one was more effective than Clarence Mackinnon, who had a winning manner and influential Scottish connections. Pidgeon too had many helpful British friends, some of them former lecturers at the summer session of Westminster Hall. He kept in touch with them very closely in the years immediately after 1925.

In some Canadian localities the disposition of Presbyterian property continued to give trouble. Ambiguities in legislation and irregularities in the taking of the vote frequently led to uncertainty, and in the absence of mutual understanding the scandal of litigation was the only recourse. The case of the Presbyterian church at Prince Rupert will serve as an example of many in which Pidgeon's advice was sought. This congregation had voted not to enter union, but was unable to secure a non-concurring pastor. It then sought to call a United Church minister, assuring him that for a time it would remain independent of either denomination. Complications mounted. The former Methodist church at Prince Rupert was alarmed at the prospect of facing competition from a minister of its own denomination. There were hints that the independent state of the congregation would not long be tolerated by the non-concurrent leadership. The liquor issue intruded. The minister concerned wanted to be loyal to the United Church, but obviously found the call attractive. This single incident raised many issues, with which Pidgeon dealt patiently as he did with scores of other equally urgent cases.

When time had disposed of most of the minor irritants, one nagging issue remained. Recognizing that the Presbyterian Church in Canada had voluntarily merged its identity, the federal United Church of Canada Act had prohibited any new denomination from taking its name. The non-concurrents, believing themselves to be the true continuing Presbyterians, proceeded to use it on all but official documents. They thereby made a public denial of the validity of Parliament's action, following it through consistently by numbering their General Assemblies in sequence from the old series. The United Church contested the claim, and the executive of the General Council decided in 1927 to take it to the Privy Council. Dr. John W. Woodside among others urged that nothing would be achieved but the reopening of old sores, and the appeal was eventually dropped. Pidgeon suggested a joint approach by the two churches to the Presbyterian Alliance on the issue, but nothing came of that either.

Meanwhile Pidgeon initiated correspondence with the non-concurring denomination in an effort to settle outstanding questions. At first the response was hesitant, but conversations were at last opened in 1932. Negotiations continued for five years, issuing in an agreement that had surely been inevitable all along. Each side simply admitted the inability of the other to accept its point of view, and the Presbyterians were allowed to use their chosen name without prejudice to the United Church case. Since that time the two denominations have worked together amicably.

The years immediately after 1925 confronted Pidgeon with a series of difficult personal decisions. He had stayed long enough at Bloor Street that he might well think of moving. On the other hand, he felt keenly that the fruition of his plans for the church had been frustrated by the demands of the union campaign and of his moderatorial year, and he was not one to leave a task uncompleted. In 1927 developments in the congregation seemed to leave his future open. As he wrote to W. M. Birks on July 4, "The congregation had adopted a programme which was too narrow for the future I had planned for it." Officials of the American Presbyterian Church in

Montreal (part of the United Church despite its name) apparently learned of the internal crisis and approached him with a view to a call. He intended to accept, but a hasty assurance from Bloor Street that he was still needed and that his plans would not be impeded brought a last-minute change of mind.

Other invitations followed. He was asked by Union College of British Columbia, which embraced the former Westminster Hall, to resume his old chair of homiletics. He was urged to become secretary of the Board of Home Missions. In 1929 he was approached by St. Andrew's-Wesley Church in Vancouver. In 1930 the American Church in Montreal pressed a second call, and this time he was only prevented from accepting by exceptional pressure from his own congregation. In 1934 he almost accepted a call to St. James' Church, Montreal, only deciding in the nick of time that his type of ministry could not readily be handed over to another. In effect he had made up his mind to remain at Bloor Street for the rest of his active ministry.

Another decision, while less weighty, was to be equally lasting. For years the family had leased a cottage at the YMCA camp at Lake Couchiching. In the course of a canoe trip, however, Mrs. Pidgeon discovered five points jutting into Lake Muldrew "like the fingers of your left hand." The Pidgeons bought three of them in 1926, building first a small cabin for daughter Alice and then a summer home on another point. For many years the cottage was a focus of family life and a base for canoe trips, although even in Muskoka the morning study period was inviolate.

10. *Mission to the Nation*

Seldom have so many people dedicated themselves to so many causes as in the decade between the crash of 1929 and the outbreak of the Second World War. The depression caused bitterness and disillusionment, but enough of the optimism of the twenties remained that the disillusionment led not to fatalism but to a confident search for alternatives to a discredited social order. Discontent was general, but so was the assurance that, with the right key, men could unlock the door to utopia. Hence there was an abundance of movements, programmes, panaceas and ideologies, of great variety but all taken very seriously by those who promoted them. Only in this period — so desperate, so hopeful and sometimes so zany—could the Kingdom of God have been promoted by means of a chain letter. The decade was marked by extremes of revolution and counter-revolution, of recklessness and paralyzing fright, but whatever their differences or their idiosyncrasies, people shared an acute awareness of the world around them.

The depression came as a particular shock to Canadians, who had not quite emerged from the Victorian era and who imagined that their social fabric was immune to sudden or unpredictable changes. Even the church union issue had been fought on a largely nineteenth-century battleground, with the evolutionary idealism of Tennyson and Browning running foul of the clan spirit of an earlier generation of immigrants. In the thirties, however, young theological pro-

118

fessors began to enlist in the class struggle, and the old slogans of social reform were turned against the virtuous as well as the wicked rich. For the first time in Canadian history the church had to contend not merely with sin and indifference but with the denial of its primary axioms of faith and morality. Those who valued the evangelical tradition that had shaped the nation's character sought feverishly to repair its foundations.

Even before the economic crash one crusade had begun to take shape. This was a movement for world peace, to be achieved through disarmament and techniques of international order. Throughout the twenties, statesmen were discussing means of preserving peace, but public interest quickened noticeably towards the close of the decade. People were no longer certain that they had won a war to end war, for recurring crises reminded them that the threat of military action was still an important diplomatic weapon. On the other hand, optimism about human capabilities suggested that, with concerted effort, war might be abolished as slavery and child labour had been. In Canada there was a special factor. Energies that had been channelled into the church union movement could now be diverted to other causes.

Interest in international peace came naturally to George Pidgeon, although he was never a pacifist. For thirty years he had been deeply engaged in controversy, first on behalf of moral reform and then for church union, but his own disposition had grown steadily more eirenic. As a young disciple of MacVicar, he had undoubtedly relished the prospect of serving in a holy war against vice and entrenched corruption. Even in Streetsville days, however, study of St. John's Gospel had led him to place on the reconciling power of Christ an emphasis that would grow with the years. It

was this, not the zest for energetic action that had characterized his youth, that interested him in the reunion of the
church. Controversy had been only an incidental and unfortunate aspect of the union movement, and once the first
objective had been attained, he inevitably turned to other
ways of bringing people together.

In 1928 he became a member of a local World Unity Council that sought, according to a letter from John Herman
Randall on October 28, "through the co-operation of our
leading scholars in church and university, the mental attitude out of which may come, at length, the intelligent international mind." In 1930 he preached twice in Cleveland as
part of an international exchange sponsored by the World
Alliance for International Friendship Through the Churches.
Many meetings over the next year culminated in a series of
rallies for disarmament sponsored by churches, labour unions
and other groups. Reinhold Niebuhr was the chief speaker
at the Toronto meeting in Massey Hall on October 26, 1931,
and Pidgeon addressed a gathering in Cleveland on October
31.

Then as now, peace movements were suspected of sub-
versive tendencies. Various prominent Canadians found
reasons for declining to speak, and even the presence of
Premier George S. Henry on the platform at Massey Hall did
not induce the police to relax the vigilance with which they
followed the activities of the committee. In more recent years
we have become accustomed to reckless accusations of disloyalty, but in 1931 respectable citizens were surprised and
shocked to find themselves under suspicion for action conscientiously taken. Principal William L. Grant of Upper
Canada College, who chaired the Toronto rally, wrote to
Pidgeon on October 30, "The way in which the Police get
people like you and me mixed up with Communists is a little

disheartening, though also rather amusing." Pidgeon and his colleagues were in no danger of arrest, but the incident was symptomatic of an uncertainty about the nature of loyalty in a democracy that was to characterize the entire decade.

As yet, however, whispered suspicions of disloyalty were no more than a minor irritant. The peace movement was widely although often passively approved by the public, and church leaders were almost unanimous in their support. Pidgeon was especially delighted to find himself working closely with members of other churches and even other faiths. Rabbi Maurice N. Eisendrath was an active supporter of the peace movement. Archbishop Neil MacNeil, with whom Pidgeon had earlier worked in Vancouver, assured Roman Catholic sympathy, although he felt that he could not co-operate publicly. As co-chairman with Harry Emerson Fosdick of the sponsoring committee, Pidgeon was also associated with such well-known Americans as Jane Addams, Norman Thomas and Rabbi Stephen S. Wise.

The disarmament campaign of 1931 was one of the last occasions when supporters of peace could meet on a single platform. Hitler's rise to power in 1933 broke the unity of the movement irreparably. Social idealists, who had hitherto been united in seeking international understanding, now had to choose between their hatred for fascism and their love of peace. Conservatives generally withdrew their support for fear of compromising their loyalty in the face of Nazi threats of aggression. Agitation against war was increasingly left to doctrinaire pacifists. Believing that Hitler had to be resisted, Pidgeon ceased to take part in public movements for peace, although on several occasions he defended the right of Christian pacifists to state their point of view.

More controversial than peace, in the early thirties, was the demand for radical changes in the economic system.

There was nothing new in the suggestion that Christian morality requires a more equal division of property than had been customary under capitalism. This had been part of the programme of the reform group within the church for many years, and Pidgeon had made some strong attacks on capitalist exploiters in British Columbia. The reformers had been limited in their demands, however, calling only for responsible and humanitarian administration of the existing order, and distinguishing between enlightened and rapacious promoters. Most of them had close friends who were successful businessmen, and looked to them for financial help and moral backing in their enterprises.

Now, however, the demand for justice took on a more strident tone. The Fellowship for a Christian Social Order, representing a radical wing of ministers and laymen, specified socialism as the economic system most in harmony with the gospel. A group in the Toronto Conference pressed for the equalization of ministerial salaries. In the universities, thoughtful Christians almost automatically took up political positions well to the left of centre. The new generation of radicals cared little for the sensibilities of Christian businessmen, who in turn often chose not to distinguish pink from red. Sympathy was distinctly lacking on both sides. Wealthy congregations were often brutal in their treatment of ministers suspected of economic heresy, while would-be martyrs were sometimes deliberately provocative in their attacks on the integrity of the entire business community.

Political radicalism was more conspicuous in the United Church than in any other denomination, not only among the rank and file, but even at headquarters. Dr. W. B. Creighton, editor of the *New Outlook*, was repeatedly accused by conservatives of turning the denominational organ into a "red propaganda-sheet." Reports of the Board of Evangel-

ism and Social Service consistently urged the socialization of
the Canadian economy. Dr. Ernest Thomas, one of the secretaries of the board, was a favourite target of business
critics. Although politically far from an extremist, he was
unable to discuss any aspect of the Christian gospel without
turning it into a social manifesto. Frequently taking their
cue from him, area conferences and even the General Council passed a series of resolutions committing the church to
a fairly advanced social position, and a minority would have
gone even further. During these depression years, the presentation of an Evangelism and Social Service report to any
church court was the recognized signal for a debate on the
economic system.

The radical group achieved one of its greatest successes
at the Toronto Conference of 1933. The conference committee on Evangelism and Social Service presented a series of
reports, of which the second dealt with economic matters.
This report called on the conference to declare:

It is our belief that the application of the principles of
Jesus to economic conditions would mean the end of the
Capitalistic System. . . . Our contention is that Capital
. . . should be owned and operated instead, not for private
gain, but in the service of the general good.

Coming down to particulars, the report listed the socialization of banks, natural resources, transportation and other
services and industries as ideals to be achieved in a Christian society. As immediate steps, it advocated social insurance, including old age assistance, unemployment insurance
and minimum wage provisions, and it ended with a plea
for the protection of primary producers.

After attempts at amendment, the report as a whole was
adopted, Pidgeon and fifty-five others registering their dis-
sent. On the minority statement Pidgeon's name came first,
followed by those of Richard Roberts, J. R. P. Sclater and

W. Harold Young. The dissenters insisted on their "abhorrence of the abuses which have grown up under the present social order" and their "conviction of the necessity of radical social readjustment." They added, however, that "declarations of this character filled with generalizations on debatable issues and with proposals the implications of which few of us understand are unworthy of a Church which accepts full responsibility for its utterances and their consequences," and concluded that a church claiming to be catholic "should not be asked to commit herself to even the apparent support of any political party."

The misgivings of responsible leaders of the church can readily be understood. One of the weaknesses of United Church practice has been its tendency to give undue prominence to committee reports and to expressions of opinion by church courts. Committees of Evangelism and Social Service tend to be composed largely of people recruited for their special interest in a few causes, and resolutions are too often addressed to no one in particular. Reformers of the thirties would have been wiser if they had paid more attention to the education of the membership of the church, and less to zealous attempts to get resolutions passed. Their success in church courts affected the attitude of the business community to the United Church more than it did that of most United Churchmen to social issues. Thus it had a somewhat fraudulent aspect. Those who regretted the flood of resolutions included some, like Roberts, who were in sympathy with most of their aims, although others were far to the right.

Pidgeon undoubtedly dissented from the content of the resolutions, for like most reformers of the evangelical school, he was essentially a conservative in economics. There was nothing in this attitude inconsistent with his earlier enthusi-

asm for social reform. Conscious of a mission to seek and
save the lost, evangelicals have always been eager to improve
the lot of the dispossessed, and so have fought vigorously
for the removal of economic abuses. On the other hand, their
emphasis on the conversion of the individual has led them to
distrust all forms of collectivism and, indeed, to be sceptical
of all techniques of social reconstruction. Throughout his
career Pidgeon maintained that the choice of an economic
system is of little importance in comparison with the integrity of the men who run it, and despite his own generosity,
and his constant readiness to help people in need, there can
be little doubt that moral depravity distressed him more
than material poverty. Holding such views, he had little
in common with the radicals of the thirties, but there were
other and more personal reasons for his opposition to them.

Having done so much to bring the United Church into
being, Pidgeon was more sensitive than most to the fragility
of the new organism. The uniting groups were no longer
strangers to each other, but in the early thirties denominational origin was still taken very seriously when church offi-
cers were elected or ministers were called. The depression
impressed upon church members their interdependence in
need, and the mobilization of resources to provide relief for
the drought-stricken west did more than any other single
factor to stimulate the self-consciousness of the United
Church. The depression also brought heartbreaking financial
reverses, however, causing severe retrenchment in all phases
of the church's work. Pidgeon, who was receiving desperate
letters from missionaries both abroad and on the frontiers,
was acutely aware of the danger of a collapse in morale.
He feared that ideological controversy might weaken the
new church irreparably. It endangered the growing together
of denominational groups, for many Presbyterians looked

upon political involvement as a Methodist specialty. It endangered the finances of the church, for wealthy men were threatening to withdraw support. Worst of all, it endangered the church's spiritual unity.

By the thirties, too, Pidgeon had come to feel that the greatest need confronting the church was neither moral reform nor social change. Everywhere he detected signs of spiritual decline and of spiritual hunger. He was pleased with the results of the union as far as they went, but he was troubled that the revival of religion for which he had pleaded as moderator had not yet come. He recognized that time was required for the knitting of diverse elements, and that denominational machinery had to be put into working order. To such delays he was reconciled, but preoccupation with economics in pulpits and church courts seemed to him intolerable trifling with deeper needs. If he sometimes became irritated with former colleagues in social reform, it was because as an evangelist he had his heart set on converting individuals.

Without doubt, the spiritual hunger was there. Throughout the church there was a widespread sense of malaise. Congregations complained of coldness in the pulpit, ministers of lack of results. The economic rigours of the depression were in part responsible for disheartenment among ministers and people, but in return the lack of spiritual assurance made these rigours even harder to bear. Despondency about the failure of conventional preaching to achieve visible results may have been one factor turning some ministers to the social gospel. Some United Church people turned in desperation to denominations apparently able to generate greater enthusiasm. Others strove to fan the embers of personal religion, and here and there they reported success. Pidgeon immersed himself in movements for personal and national evangelism.

In 1930, Canada's four largest non-Roman denominations appointed a committee to investigate the possibility of a "simultaneous movement for the evangelization of Canadian life." There was no thought at first of a joint campaign. Instead each church was to devise its own programme while consulting the others to achieve the greatest possible concentration of effort. Pidgeon was named acting chairman, and when the committee completed its organization on October 21, 1932, his position was confirmed. He could scarcely have resisted the appeal of a movement at once interdenominational, evangelistic and national.

The promotion of one simultaneous national mission was apparently the original purpose of the Inter-Church Committee. It soon became an established instrument for the co-ordination of evangelistic effort, however, with Pidgeon as its permanent chairman. In its early years it distributed literature and arranged services of Christian witness in various centres. In 1936 it arranged a series of mass rallies in cities across Canada, with Pidgeon as one of the speakers in the west. In 1937 it sponsored a conference at McMaster University, and in 1938 Pidgeon spoke at a number of Maritime centres. With the outbreak of war ambitious national campaigns became impracticable, but consultation on local projects continued.

The committee's evangelistic programme was not spectacularly successful. Efforts to obtain outstanding speakers from abroad were frustrated by failure to secure Archbishop William Temple and then by the difficulty of agreeing on a substitute. In some cities it was impossible to obtain the participation of all denominations at once. Many adherents of the social gospel were openly sceptical of the timeliness of mass rallies and services of witness: the Reverend J. W. A. Nicholson warned in a letter of September 10, 1936, that all would be "hyprocrisy and blasphemy" unless ministers would really take their place with the common people. In 1940, Dr. A. S. Tuttle was still repeating the old complaint that ministers were not preaching for a verdict. Undeterred by disappointment, Pidgeon gave to the work of the committee the careful planning of details that marked everything he did. He did not see the revival he desired, but he initiated among the Canadian churches a pattern of mutual consultation that has been extended over the years.

While mass rallies were achieving only a partial success, evangelism of a very different sort was claiming spectacular results. The auspices were new, but there was nothing new about the method. The origins of what we commonly call evangelical Christianity can be traced back to groups of Christians in the Rhineland in the late eighteenth century who shared a close personal fellowship and encouraged intimate personal witness. It is easy to find many parallels with earlier monastic and semi-monastic movements. This "conventicle" type of religion can exist either within or alongside more formally organized churches. It easily becomes ingrown and exclusive, but it can also be remarkably contagious. Indeed, the Christian church has usually expanded more successfully by taking outsiders into its fellowship than by trying to convert them in mass meetings.

During a visit to Toronto in 1931, Toyohiko Kagawa told of bringing Christians together in small groups to share experiences and strengthen each other's faith. A group of ministers was inspired to imitate his method, and although there was no attempt to reach out to the unconverted, some Canadians had a taste of the intimacy of the Christian cell group. A member of the Kagawa Fellowship, Pidgeon had also heard favourable reports of an experiment in Winnipeg along similar lines conducted by his friend John Mackay. The

Corpus Christi movement, as it was called, was an attempt on Mackay's part to recapture the experience of the New Testament church in modern terms.

Then, in 1932, a team of the Oxford Group visited Toronto, introducing a pattern of evangelism that was soon being talked about everywhere. In its essentials this was simply the classical pattern of evangelical piety, but under the direction of Frank Buchman it was presented with a professional flair that attracted members of a class usually immune to evangelistic appeals. The Oxford Group deliberately and openly appealed to the wealthy and the sophisticated. Public meetings served only to advertise its presence and make contacts. The serious work of evangelism took place in house parties, frequently at resort hotels, to which a selected group of interested people had been invited. There they were instructed in the four absolutes—purity, honesty, unselfishness and love—and initiated into such typical group practices as sharing and guidance. Sharing was the mutual confession of experiences and sins. Guidance was direct advice from God in response to prayer. It was expected that no important decisions would be taken without it and teams awaited it before determining their itineraries and issuing invitations to their private sessions. After the excitement of a team visit, those whose lives had been changed carried on the work in small permanent groups. In theory, at least, there was no central organization: the groups were to act as a leaven under no control but that of the Holy Spirit.

The response of United Church officialdom was distinctly cool. The Board of Evangelism and Social Service issued a statement to ministers, cautiously indicating features that might be helpful while pointedly warning them against inherent dangers. Dr. Creighton was unreservedly hostile in the *New Outlook*. The social action school held aloof, its point of view being represented by an equivocal but largely unfavourable analysis published by an unofficial Committee of Thirty. Many United Church ministers and laymen became active group members, however, and smouldering criticisms of headquarters occasionally burst into flame.

It is not difficult in retrospect to discover in the Oxford Group of 1932 many of the features that have made churchmen increasingly wary of involvement with its successor, Moral Re-Armament. There was the same high-pressure salesmanship advertising the benefits to be derived from the movement more effectively than the Christian gospel itself. There was the same exploitation of the names of prominent converts, and even of mere endorsement by the powerful. There was already evidence of autocratic control and of swift excommunication for any who deviated from the Buchman line. Even then the movement's propaganda was filled with vague promises about remaking nations. Even the earliest teams always seemed to contain at least one widely advertised ex-Communist.

To understand the impression made in 1932, however, we must banish from our minds the current image of Moral Re-Armament. The most controversial features of the Oxford Group were not its political implications but its sensationalism and the fear that it might break away from the churches. Tales were told of disclosures made in sessions of sharing that broke up homes and wrecked ministries. The direct line to heaven implied in guidance seemed to liberal theologians a throwback to an outgrown obscurantism. Socialist critics condemned the movement not for rightist tendencies, but for the lack of any social content in its message as well as for its special interest in the "dinnerjacket set." Defenders insisted that the leaders of the movement took all possible precautions against emotional excess, and they pleaded that most members, even of the visiting teams, were recent converts who would need time to understand all the implications of New Testament Christianity. To them the great attraction of the Oxford Group was that it was getting the spiritual results others were only talking about.

From the beginning Pidgeon worked closely with the groups. He welcomed visiting teams to his church, where the group method soon became an established feature of his ministry. From Bloor Street, he led teams to other congregations, and on occasion he took ministerial teams to other cities. He corresponded for years with people who had met him or heard of him through the groups, giving encouragement and spiritual advice. He became a recognized spokesman for the movement. Along with several other ministers, he publicly protested the attitude of the *New Outlook*, and at Buchman's request he defended the groups in a letter to the London *Times*.

It is clear from correspondence that Pidgeon was more keenly aware of the limitations of the Oxford Group than the warmth of his public support would indicate. He distrusted its tendency to rely upon a spirituality that was not always deeply rooted in the Bible, and he saw clearly the dangers inherent in some of its methods. He was delighted by its success in changing lives, however, and he was eager to retain for the church a movement that could easily become sectarian. Some leading groupers were active members of his own congregation, and he wanted to guide rather than to quench their spiritual enthusiasm.

Within a few years the uproar died away. Most people ceased to be aware of the existence of the groups, and socialites who had once publicly announced their "spiritual birthdays" pretended that they had never had religion. Among initiates, however, group activities went on for many years.

Vagaries of sensational sharing were forgotten, but meetings for meditation, Bible study and mutual counsel continued. A ministerial fellowship constituted on group lines met regularly in the Bloor Street vestry. Clergy sympathetic to the movement came to depend on inner circles of the devout for spiritual leadership in their congregations. In some churches a residue of influence remains today, and such contemporary movements as Alcoholics Anonymous imitate the methods of the groups.

11. Minister at Bloor Street

George Pidgeon's first concern at Bloor Street after union was to repair the damage caused by the constant interruptions to his work and to replace the leaders lost to the non-concurrents. Then, having made up his mind to remain with his congregation, he had the satisfaction of seeing his ministry begin to yield a harvest commensurate with his sowing. After 1930, despite many outside involvements, Bloor Street was the focus of his activities. He had decided for the pastorate early in his ministry, and now at last he would have an unimpeded opportunity to carry out his resolve. In the pastorate, too, he would be able to make his most effective contribution to the revival of religion he so much desired. He refers to the period from 1930 to 1948 as the culmination of his ministry, and it is on the basis of his pastoral work that he makes this judgment.

At one time it looked as if he had given himself to the pastorate too unstintingly. Early in 1934 he suffered a serious physical collapse. The congregation sent him south to recover, but there he was troubled for a time by severe insomnia. At this point his faith took over, and he noted later in a sermon that he had learned to take a much more relaxed approach to his work. He did not slacken his pace, but he was able to maintain his strength undiminished to the end of a ministry of thirty-three years at Bloor Street.

Like everything else he undertook, his pastoral work was thoroughly planned with definite ends in view. He had in mind a broad programme that would not only meet the needs of members of the congregation, but would also serve the area in which it was located, reaching out to affect the life of the city. He expected his congregation to support him in this programme, and after some hesitation it responded enthusiastically to his leadership.

In 1929 a friend in the ministry asked for advice on a pastoral problem. Pidgeon's reply, although bearing too closely on the specific situation to serve as a summary of his own pastoral method, gives some indication of his thinking as he approached the decisive period of his Bloor Street ministry.

First, give your full strength to your Sunday services, even if you have only half a dozen people. . . . Second, take a personal interest in the men. . . . Third, try to meet their social needs.

Preaching naturally came first. A large portion of each week still went towards the preparation of his sermons, and when he entered the pulpit he counted on at least thirty minutes of his congregation's time. Although he spoke without notes, each sermon was a finely shaped piece of craftsmanship. Pidgeon was a belated representative of a race of preachers for whom the sermon was an art-form with its own intrinsic canons of excellence. He used the same care in preparing the entire service of worship, in contrast to many preachers of his generation who regarded prayer and praise as mere preliminaries to the sermon. The lessons received special attention. He knew many passages of Scripture by heart, and would recite them to the congregation more as personal testimonies than as readings.

Many of those who heard Pidgeon referred to him as an expository preacher. He has always repudiated the title, insisting that his sermons were topical. It is difficult to accept his judgment without reserve, for the biblical content of his preaching was unmistakable. His custom was to describe a fairly long passage of Scripture, then explain it and apply it. A passage in the *Reminiscences* of Principal Clarence Mackinnon may give the clue to Pidgeon's disclaimer. Mackinnon told how in the first decade of this century people, weary of controversy, turned from doctrinal and biblical to evangelistic sermons. "Anecdotes, bits of biography, graphic stories, supplanted the dry argument and the accumulated texts."* Pidgeon's style had been formed in this period. In reaction against the rather arid speculations of the previous generation, he intended his sermons to have immediate and obvious application to the situation of his hearers. Unlike many topical preachers, however, he chose his anecdotes with serious purpose and embedded them in a carefully constructed argument from Scripture. "Gospel preaching . . . requires plain, straight telling,"† he once wrote, and his own preaching exemplified his advice.

Pidgeon's reputation as a preacher cannot be explained by any novelty in his message. During the years when he was in his prime, some ministers were becoming known as prophets of a new gospel of social change, while others were wrestling with questions raised by literary and scientific critics of the Bible. Although sympathetic to those who explored new areas of thought, Pidgeon made little use of their themes in the pulpit. His message was that of the nineteenth-century evangelists, adorned with literary grace and purged of obscurantism but still directed to the spiritual rebirth and moral growth of the individual.

There can be no doubt of the powerful impression made by these sermons on those who heard them. One secret of their power was their importance to the man who composed and delivered them. Some were classics, preached on many

---

*P. 173.
†*The Indwelling Christ*, p. 83.

occasions and still remembered by name: two of the more memorable were "The Prayer of Faith," based upon John 15: 7 and inspired by an incident at Nelson, B.C., and "Kadesh-barnea," an exposition of Deuteronomy 1: 19. Pidgeon valued his sermons so highly that he put into them only material that seemed to him significant and authoritative. He quoted serious works of literature rather than the trivial illustrations found in so many books of sermons, and he frequently referred to incidents that had been decisive either in his own experience or in that of others. His attitude to the Bible reinforced the gravity of his preaching. "He never bowdlerizes the Scriptures," his predecessor wrote of him. "He seeks to declare the whole counsel of God as revealed by His Word."[*]

Pidgeon regarded his sermons as important because he himself expected much of them. He took with the utmost seriousness the spiritual problems of the people before him, and he believed that the sermon might be the means of resolving them. Therefore each sermon took on a note of urgency that communicated itself to the listeners. "If I can make Romans 8 one of our spiritual treasures," he said in introducing one sermon, "this service will be memorable all our days."[†] Many of his services were long remembered.

The Bloor Street sanctuary was redesigned in the early years of Pidgeon's ministry. A semi-circle of pews closely grouped around a central pulpit had the effect at once of exalting the preacher's office and of transforming the congregation into an enlarged fellowship group. The amphitheatre style, so well adapted to his quiet and thoughtful manner of speaking, did not long survive his retirement. It has long been out of fashion, along with the sombre woodwork and gilded organ pipes that

---

[*]*Seventy Years at Bloor Street, A History of Bloor Street United Church, Toronto, 1887-1957* (Toronto, Joint Board of Bloor Street United Church, 1957), p. 16.
[†]*The Indwelling Christ,* p. 121.

commonly went with it. After experimenting with medieval chancels, however, Protestant churches are once again seeking in their architecture to suggest the intimacy of the family of God.

With preaching always went teaching, and a current tendency to distinguish the two received little encouragement. Pidgeon took little active part in young people's work at Bloor Street, but all his congregations were known as centres of Christian education. His secret was in securing first-rate leaders and entrusting the responsibility to them. A series of assistant ministers took charge of work among young people, while deaconesses dealt with the special problems of single women in the area. Pidgeon appeared at the occasional meeting, identifying himself with the various phases of the congregation's life and making himself available to anyone who wanted to consult him.

He interpreted Christian education broadly, opening his church building to varied social and athletic activities. Earlier in the Chapter, there was a reference to a request for advice from a fellow minister. The particular problem troubling the correspondent was that his young people were getting into trouble at a local dance hall. Pidgeon's advice was to persuade the young people to hire the hall and to arrange dancing on their own terms. This attitude, unusually liberal in 1929, reflected a realism about human nature that tempered what might otherwise have been an excessively pious approach to the problems of the modern urban congregation.

The full-bodied programme of preaching, teaching and social activity that kept the Bloor Street building in use throughout the week was only secondarily for the benefit of the members of the church. Pidgeon was primarily the pastor of a congregation, but a Christian congregation, as he conceived it, was not a static fellowship of believers but an expendable missionary cell. From his headquarters in the pulpit, he was eager to reach out into the surrounding city, and he pressed his people to reach out with him.

Sermons were inevitably his most effective means of making contacts with outsiders, for it was from the pulpit that he most freely spoke his mind. However conscientiously he might seek to provide all the ingredients of a modern church programme, it was his ability as a preacher that first attracted people to the church. The institution became important only in the next stage, when those who had come to hear him were ready to look to the church for help in solving their problems and broadening their interests. The church's location, in an area no longer predominantly residential but not quite downtown, made it ideal as a preaching centre, without depriving it of a core of solid congregational support. Single roomers with white collars were especially conspicuous in the streets running off Bloor.

The University of Toronto was not far away, and many of its students found lodgings in the Annex. Pidgeon made a special effort to attract them, choosing the topics of many of his sermons with their interests in mind. A friend who knew the university in the thirties recalls that United Church students with intellectual tastes were attracted by the incisive sermons of Richard Roberts at Sherbourne, that those in search of sensation were likely to find it elsewhere, but that the largest group listened to Pidgeon. They were attracted, he said, by Pidgeon's knack of dealing with questions "that were in your mind but you didn't know it."

The impression that he made on students was not entirely due to his ability as a preacher. There was some quality in his character that made students feel that they could trust him, an integrity that led inquirers to seek his advice even when they regarded his views as a little out of date. It was his custom to pay an annual visit to a co-operative student residence across the street from the Bloor Street manse. The calls were always very formal, for neither he nor the students had much to say to each other, but they helped to establish his position on the campus. He surprised and pleased members of a dental fraternity by giving the same attention to their house, and in return they annually filled a section of his church. A tribute that particularly touched him was a request that he should continue his special sermons to students of Knox College even after union.

Pidgeon seized upon any honourable method that would enable him to extend his influence. The morning services at Bloor Street were broadcast from 1929, and his radio contacts initiated him into an informal chaplaincy to a large corresponding congregation. Many of those who wrote had complex personal problems, and some were obviously pathetic souls who sensed his readiness to take time to notice them. A number of letters indicate that people whose religious training had been narrowly conservative had unusual confidence in his ability to help them in periods of intellectual adjustment. Meanwhile, his Sunday School columns and his books continued to extend his pulpit ministry.

The Bloor Street congregation was constantly urged to look outward. It had always been missionary-minded, and he encouraged its interest. The church corresponded with adopted missionaries overseas, and at one time during the depression relieved the Board of Home Missions of its entire responsibility for aid to the churches of Cochrane Presbytery in northern Ontario. Pidgeon also involved the congregation in less obvious forms of Christian outreach. He established a tradition of reporting from the pulpit upon every important conference he attended, and he encouraged the congregation to make friendly approaches to the Jewish community and to other denominations.

Pidgeon's ministry at Bloor Street had an intensely personal quality, as he was forcibly reminded whenever he thought of leaving. Organizations multiplied, tasks were readily assigned to others, but everything about the church had his stamp on it. Such a close and constant interrelation of minister and people was obviously possible only in a long ministry. Pidgeon was carrying on a Presbyterian tradition of permanence in the pastorate already established at Bloor Street by his pre- decessor's ministry of twenty-five years. Ministries of such length are uncommon in the twentieth century. A novel approach or a fund of anecdotes may keep a minister going for a few years, but shoddiness in character or message will eventually show up. Pidgeon had the staying power to make the tradition work, holding the respect of the intelligent and the progressive to the very end of his ministry.

Those who have worked under him insist that, despite his unquestioned position as pastor of the congregation, Pidgeon was never an autocrat. Important decisions were taken only after thorough discussion in staff meetings, and if it was the minister's opinion that necessarily prevailed, no one felt that his advice had been undervalued. And while the total pattern of congregational life was unquestionably of Pidgeon's making, each staff member was left free to make his own peculiar con- tribution to it. The result was neither one-man control nor rule by committee, but a sum of complementary individual influences. His relations with his assistants—to whom he always referred as colleagues—were particularly happy. He chose them with care and then allowed them to grow in line with their own abilities and inclinations, although he left them in no doubt about the quality of service he expected.

If Bloor Street was somehow different from most churches,

it was because the pastor always insisted on excellence. He would have only the ablest and most consecrated young ministers as assistants. The choir and organist had to excel, and only music of the first quality was to be sung. No matter what office in the congregation fell vacant, he looked around for the best possible person to fill it. In such cases prestige did not count. With a keen eye for latent talent, he found positions in which college deans and ordinary workmen served with distinction. Of course no slacker could have organized a congregation so efficiently. The excellence that characterized every aspect of the Bloor Street programme reflected the pastor's own dedication to his job. Every sermon was carefully composed, every meeting prepared for, every detail planned.

Meticulous attention to important matters was possible only because Pidgeon was able to forget what he regarded as unimportant. No man can do everything, and it may have been the effects of his breakdown in 1934 that gave him his exceptional ability to distinguish between what he had to do and what he could safely leave to others. As a former assistant remarked, "his congregation was organized for maximum effectiveness, not for maximum activity." He was always busy, but he was never hurried, never distracted, never occupied with trivialities.

The distinction of Pidgeon's ministry was only in its quality, not in its type. There was nothing unusual in any of his methods. He made Bloor Street a centre of Christian education in an era when everyone was emphasizing Christian education; he took social and athletic activities into his programme when gymnasia were in vogue. The mainstay of his pastoral strategy was not the application of techniques of counselling or group dynamics, both of which he would have rejected as forms of personal manipulation, but diligence in the familiar Protestant pattern of preaching and visitation. No more either was his success the result of extraordinary charm or of personal magnetism. Pidgeon is a shy man who impresses with his kindliness, but he does not readily make conversation with strangers or sparkle in a group. Even Oxford Group colleagues, who used Christian names as a matter of principle, did not venture to address letters "Dear George."

In the end the remarkable effectiveness of his ministry can be explained only by the depth and solidity of its spiritual foundations. Some men have undoubtedly had more brilliant ministries. Some have been more contemporary, more incisive, more sensitive to emerging ideas. Few have been so rich in the wisdom that is acquired through constant prayer and meditation on the Scriptures. The habit of ordering his life through daily communion with God gave Pidgeon a poise and a presence that more than compensated for any lack of dramatic impact. This enabled him to wait out crises in the assurance that the right answers would be given. As he moved among his people, he made them aware of another dimension of being, and they responded by accepting his conviction that only the best can fitly be offered to God.

12. "That They All May Be One"

As the inevitability of another world war grew more apparent, churchmen everywhere sensed the urgency of establishing a common understanding that would survive the struggle. In 1914 the churches had all too readily allowed themselves to become recruiting agencies for the warring nations, leaving a residue of distrust and disillusionment that discredited Christianity in the minds of many idealists. In the years just before 1939, a flurry of ecumenical activity witnessed to the determination of Christian leaders to maintain friendly contacts through no matter what emergency.

In this activity Pidgeon played a role of some importance. After several years during which most of his energies had been engaged elsewhere, he plunged into a period of intense involvement in the ecumenical movement. He could now feel that the pattern of his ministry at Bloor Street was well established. The spiritual state of the nation showed some signs of recovery from the apparent aridity of the early thirties. He was free for a new venture.

There had, in fact, been no real interruption in the concern for Christian reintegration that had carried him through the horrors of the union controversy. Almost from the beginning of his ministry, most of his outside activities had been interdenominational in scope and after 1925 his interest in joint projects was even more conspicuous. In 1929, for example, he attended a conference on church union sponsored by a group of prominent American churchmen who called

143

themselves the Christian Herald Association. He was appointed a delegate to the Faith and Order conference at Lausanne in 1927, and although he was unable to go, he became in 1932 a member of its continuation committee. In 1936 he attended an ecumenical consultation at Princeton, New Jersey, and in the same year he took part in informal conversations on "The Recovery of Fellowship" with Canadian Anglicans and Presbyterians.

A period of even more intense ecumenical activity was ushered in by a coincidence. Two important world conferences were scheduled for 1937: one at Oxford on the Life and Work of the church, the other at Edinburgh on its Faith and Order. Learning that Dr. and Mrs. Pidgeon were planning a vacation trip to Scotland that summer, United Church leaders asked him to represent his church at both conferences. Economy was important in that darkest year of the depression, although in view of his known interest and ecumenical experience it seems inconceivable that he could have been left off the list in any case. At Oxford, where he was an associate delegate, he reported that representatives "came together feeling an agglomeration" but that an intense desire for unity soon appeared. The dark feature of the conference was the absence of the German delegation, which could not get permission to leave their country. From Oxford the Pidgeons went on to Edinburgh, salvaging what they could of their intended vacation en route at Llandudno and in the Lake District.

For Pidgeon, at sixty-five, Oxford and Edinburgh marked the beginning of a new ecumenical career. He became a member of the continuation committee appointed by the two conferences to inaugurate a World Council of Churches. He was named also a member of a North American committee of fourteen, and chairman of the continuation committee for

Canada. A year of constant consultation led to a further meeting in 1938 at Utrecht, where he took part in the drafting of the constitution of the World Council. The outbreak of war in 1939 prevented any immediate further steps towards formal organization. From its Geneva office, however, the World Council "in process of formation" was able to maintain Christian contacts unbroken across battle lines and to provide relief in some cases of desperate need, thus demonstrating the success of last-minute efforts to cement the church's fellowship against the coming ordeal.

At home Pidgeon's position put him in the thick of discussions leading up to the formation of the Canadian Council of Churches in 1944. Indeed, nothing offers more convincing evidence of the importance of his contribution to mutual understanding among Canadian churches than the composition of this council. The Inter-Church Committee for the Evangelization of Canadian Life, which he had guided since 1930, became its Department of Evangelism. The Christian Social Council of Canada, of which he had once been chairman, also became an important part of the council. Consciously or unconsciously, he had spent much of his lifetime laying the foundations upon which an ecumenical structure could be built. Even activities that seemed to have little to do with unity took their place in the emerging pattern.

With the new order his chairmanship of the old joint committee lapsed, and he was glad enough to step down. As an executive member of the Canadian Council he maintained his old associations, however, advising on finance and sharing in the planning of a series of university missions. In conjunction with Dr. W. J. Gallagher, he also prepared a Lenten booklet issued by the council in 1943.

Meanwhile another form of ecumenical action was taking even more of his attention. For many years he had been a member of the Alliance of Reformed Churches Holding the Presbyterian System (now Order). In 1938 he was elected to a one-year term as chairman of its Western Section, and for the next five years he convened its programme committee. He brought to the Alliance his old passion for Christian unity along with a new urgency for its greater realization. Oxford and Edinburgh had rekindled his enthusiasm for unity, but he had been disturbed at these conferences by the comparative poverty of Reformed contributions to the discussions. Under his chairmanship, Presbyterians would be challenged to pull their weight in the ecumenical movement.

For five years, therefore, a series of papers on "The Reformed Contribution to the Ecumenical Movement" was a regular feature on the agenda of the Alliance. Leading theologians of the United States and Canada were pressed into service, and the convener of the committee saw to it that several of the papers dealt with the ecumenical significance of The United Church of Canada. By 1948 the results of Pidgeon's regime were apparent. Representatives of Reformed churches throughout the world convened at Geneva that year to clarify their position on many ecumenical issues, basing most of their discussions on the papers prepared by the Western Section. Many of the delegates went on to the first Assembly of the World Council of Churches at Amsterdam later that year, presumably better aware of the ecumenical implications of their own historic position. Pidgeon took part in the Geneva consultation and in planning sessions for Amsterdam at New York, but he was unable to remain in Europe for the inauguration of the World Council.

Although he was always an expert organizer who took pleasure in planning details for utmost effectiveness, his interest in the ecumenical movement sprang from something more than a desire to co-ordinate Christian forces throughout the world. His concern was for the unity of Christ's people, and he saw this as coming about only by the sharing of treasures now parcelled out among many communions and isolated national groups. Towards the realization of this unity, the merger of a few similar denominations could be no more than a feeble first step: Christ's prayer was "that they all may be one." At one of the sessions of the Oxford Conference he scribbled in his notebook, "In Canada our need is unity . . . not one element left out; if one group left out an essential factor is gone." Not only each group but each facet of Christian truth and experience should be blended into the unity to come.

Is Pidgeon naïve in his confidence that union will come about not by compromise or surrender but by a process of mutual sharing? Perhaps, but his conviction is firmly rooted in Scripture as read and pondered over a lifetime. He believes in union because he believes that God wills it, rejecting the suggestion of spiritual unity without bodily expression as foreign to the thought of the New Testament. "Do not let your diversities break up God's unities," he once wrote, "you sin against Him when you do it."* He believes in union because he regards all Christian experiences as essentially one:

The one necessity which the apostles stressed everywhere was that this fellowship in Christ should be unbroken. Differences of race or language or colour or class, distance or occupation or degree of culture, simply did not touch the central reality of Christian experience, namely the indwelling of the living Christ.†

Most of all he believes in union because the Trinity is one. Valuing the Epistle of the Ephesians highly in his later years for its clear statement of the solidarity of the human race with Christ in redemption, he turned to the Gospel according to

*The Indwelling Christ, p. 175.
†The Communion of Saints, p. 8f.

Saint John for its insistence upon the "complete identity of will and purpose between the Father and Son, unity of heart and mind and will for Divine ends."* The wider union to which he dedicated himself would be a reflection of the eternal unity of God's own Being.

To a surprising extent the present pattern of ecumenical Christianity was moulded during the most trying years of the Second World War. There was a constant stream of ecumenical traffic under the most hazardous conditions as Christian leaders of the belligerent nations met in Geneva, and as Christians of neutral citizenship took messages back and forth. Even in North America, freedom of movement was curtailed. Pidgeon's many trips to the United States on ecumenical business meant a constant battle against exchange regulations, and there were times when visits were possible only because the American committee was willing to put up his train fare.

Meanwhile pastoral work at Bloor Street had to take account of the war and of the enlistment of members of the congregation. A Red Cross unit was organized in the church. The younger women of the Kirk Club adopted the mine-sweeper *Brabant*. The Woman's Association and the Kirk Club collected relief supplies, sending food and clothing to British nursery schools, Christmas boxes to homeless children, servicemen and prisoners of war. Pidgeon regularly wrote letters to those who had enlisted from the congregation, and later his morning sermons were printed for distribution to them.

He believed in the war and gave tireless support to the congregation's effort, but he detested the wartime hysteria that threatened the church's prophetic voice. He rejected the pacifist position, but he pleaded that the loyalty of pacifists to their country should be recognized. In 1942, when an attempt was made to commit the United Church to the con-

---

*From a sermon on John 1.

scriptionist line, he opposed it on grounds similar to those
which had led him to protest against socialist resolutions
during the depression. His views on the relation of the church
to the war were expressed in some detail in a Christmas
message that was drafted in 1939 for the Canadian committee
of the World Council of Churches:

While we affirm our membership in civil society as of divine
appointment and accept our civil duties as of God, our primary
citizenship is in his supranational kingdom. . . . Without
abating a jot of our condemnation for the greed for possession
and the lust for power, without relaxing for a moment our
hold on liberty and justice, we will not let the Church become
the organ of any civil society, including our own. . . . Our
membership is in the Great Church, the Church of all ages
and of all lands, including our fellow-Christians in enemy
countries.

It may have been Pidgeon's refusal to allow the church to
be made a mere instrument for the war effort that led his
congregation to extend its humanitarian activities into the
post-war period. Relief projects went on as before, now
directed to the rescue of those made homeless by the war,
and a number of refugees were brought to Canada under
congregational sponsorship.

Despite the strains of war the pastor showed few signs
of declining vigour. He found a new field of interest in
educational policy, then under consideration in Ontario by
the Hope Commission. Like his old teacher MacVicor, he
believed that religion should be an integral part of the school
curriculum, and he was greatly pleased when the Ontario
government made more liberal provision for it. In 1946 he
was helping to plan a university Christian mission. In 1947
he was a member of a Committee for Religious Tolerance
chaired by John R. Mott. In 1948 he attacked Premier
Drew for his liquor policy, and despite his own tradition of

Conservatism urged United Church members to vote the government out. This was an active enough programme for a man in his seventies.

Here and there, however, one can detect symptoms of slowing down. He sat on almost as many committees as ever, but increasingly his role was that of elder statesman and adviser. He was asked to open meetings with prayer, his advice was sought and his experience was valued, but he began to divest himself of executive responsibility. Increasingly he had occasion to recall the past. In 1944, his jubilee year in the ministry, he summed up his career in the sermon "Fifty Years Trying." In 1945 he celebrated his thirtieth year at Bloor Street. Kenneth Forbes painted his portrait, and Dr. Sidney Smith presented a cheque for more than five thousand dollars to begin a George C. Pidgeon Fund for postgraduate work at Emmanuel College. In 1947 the University of Toronto conferred its Doctorate of Laws. Then on June 30, 1948, he retired from the active pastorate to become minister emeritus of Bloor Street Church. He was seventy-six.

Despite his advanced age at retirement, he was not ready to give up. Those who rushed to sign him up for preaching engagements were told that he had agreed to deliver a series of lectures in homilectics at Emmanuel that fall. In 1949 and 1950 he visited the western theological colleges of the United Church. Questions had been raised in General Council about their efficiency and about the need of retaining all of them, and he was made chairman of a special committee. In the course of this tour of duty, he gave the W. H. Smith Memorial lectures in homiletics at Union College of British Columbia.

In retirement, Pidgeon even found a cause to which he could give himself with the determination and fire of his earlier years. He had expected great benefits from the new courses of religious instruction authorized in Ontario in 1947, but the initial results were disappointing. The Ontario act placed the initiative for starting classes in religious subjects on the ministers themselves, and comparatively few had done so. Further investigation showed that in almost every province similar opportunities were being missed. Pidgeon took to the road again as a campaigner, crossing Canada three times in an effort to rouse local committees. His mission had a very specific purpose. His aim was not to secure new legislation but to press the churches to make more use of existing laws. Neither did he suggest that the schools should undertake to teach children the doctrines of the Christian faith. He regards such instruction as the responsibility of the church, but he believes that in a country shaped by the Bible the state cannot afford to let its citizens be ignorant of its contents.

Pastoral work came to an end, but preaching and writing continued unabated. Pidgeon was in constant demand for anniversaries and other special occasions. When the United Church celebrated its twenty-fifth anniversary in 1950, he conducted the service in the Maple Leaf Gardens. He dedicated a centre for Christian adult education at Five Oaks in 1955. He comforted a congregation at Woodbridge immediately after Hurricane Hazel in 1957. A church service under his leadership became a regular feature of Toronto's annual pilgrimage to admire autumn leaves. From 1949 to 1960 he contributed a column to the weekly church page of the Toronto *Telegram*. Books continued to appear. Immediately upon retirement he began to set down his recollections of the church union movement, publishing them under the title *The United Church of Canada* in 1950. Other works, *The Way of Salvation* and a Lenten booklet *From Fear to Faith*, which were devotional in tone, also appeared. In his preaching and writing, Pidgeon was drawing on many years of study and meditation, but in neither was he content merely to rephrase old thoughts. Having found Paul's messages to churches especially helpful for pastoral preaching, he now used his greater leisure to study John's conception of the love of God.

Age brought bereavements and losses, but it brought satisfaction too. Fire destroyed the newly decorated sanctuary of Bloor Street Church in 1953, and with shifts in Toronto's population, the question of moving or uniting with another church was inevitably in some people's minds. Soon, however, the congregation rebuilt their sanctuary on a larger scale than before. A dwelling north of the church was purchased in 1954 and renamed the George C. Pidgeon House. In 1959 he was called upon to unveil a window in the new sanctuary that recognized those, including himself, who had helped to bring The United Church of Canada into being. In 1955 he had the special satisfaction of being recognized by McGill with an honorary Doctorate of Divinity. As with his earlier Montreal D.D. in course, he was the first Canadian recipient. On his ninetieth birthday, leading representatives of The United Church of Canada came to congratulate him. Surrounded by flowers, he accepted the homage due to a wise and good man.

13. *Whole Counsel*

Born less than five years after Confederation, Dr. George Pidgeon maintains in the heart of Toronto a style of life fundamentally unchanged from that of a past generation. Although he has always kept in touch with the times, reading up on the latest ideas and adopting the latest methods, one feels that time has not essentially affected him. The scale of values by which he lives is not greatly different from that which he came to accept under the influence of home and church at New Richmond, although experience and travel have broadened his horizon. He strikes the visitor as a man out of the current fashion, a last eminent Victorian living in a secular society that is not his accustomed environment. Listening to him one hears again after a lapse of years a vocabulary of courtesy and piety that no longer comes naturally to most people.

Throughout his career, Pidgeon has made his reputation as an effective leader of existing movements, rather than as the originator of new ones. The impulse of moral and social reform, the church union enterprise and the ecumenical movement all had taken recognizable shape before he became associated with them. His function was to make them effective within his sphere of influence. Even in giving leadership he has seldom attracted a devoted group of personal followers. In this century of movements, a number of churchmen have made themselves centres of controversy, generating both fanatical loyalty and bitter dislike. Pidgeon has never been surrounded by a claque, and he would never have tolerated one. He places a high value on personal leadership, but only when the follower is free to be himself. Besides, his own temper is conservative. He distrusts the extremism associated with conspicuous innovators, and he believes that most important changes are made by those who are not enamoured of change for its own sake.

If he has not attracted disciples, he has had many admirers and—more significantly—imitators. A former assistant has said that whenever he is at a loss for a ready solution to a problem he asks himself quickly, "How would Dr. Pidgeon do it?" The secret lies, perhaps, in the rigid standards of excellence he has always set for himself, or in the "undeviating perspective" with which the same person credited him. He prepared himself for his ministry to the point where he never allowed himself to be caught by surprise, and he therefore never made a fool of himself.

By itself, however, excellence is a cold quality. Pidgeon's was formed by the constant practice of personal meditation and self-discipline. His was a consecrated determination to excel, transmuting natural ambition into a resolve to make his life, and everything connected with it, the worthiest possible offering to God. The result was a quality of personal holiness that could not be obscured by controversy or compromised by active involvement in debatable public issues. Inhibited in contacts with today's man of the world by an inbred Victorian sense of decorum, he communicates a saintliness so transparently genuine that none can fail to be affected by it.

If Pidgeon is to be called a saint, however, he must be called one in terms of the puritan and evangelical tradition in which he was raised. His sanctity is that of the practical Christian who fulfils his vocation in a world of limited possibilities. Holiness of life never seemed to him incompatible with public agitation or, indeed, with the use of private influence to secure what he regarded as righteous ends. In this, however, he is not greatly different from the saints of any denomination. Genuine saints, as distinct from those whose lives were invented or embellished by pious imagination, have always been known for their toughness. Among medieval saints his most obvious comparison is with Bernard of Clairvaux: both evangelical preachers immersed in the Bible; both instruments of change while hostile to novelty; both at once men of action and men of the study and cloister.

More than almost any other man, the saint requires tact if he is to be helpful to others. It is not easy to be holy, and the strain of striving is apt to betray itself in a stridency that repels, or in a brittle edginess that always seems to put others in the wrong. When militancy is joined to sanctity, the difficulties are multiplied, for it is all too easy for zeal to degenerate into fanaticism or ruthlessness. Pidgeon gives the impression of being on easy terms with his piety. In public campaigns he smote vigorously but without rancour. As a pastor he invited the confidence of many whose pattern of living differed markedly from his. His own vigorous self-discipline seemed to give him an unusual sympathy with the difficulties of the undisciplined, and people sought his help in coping with a great variety of disorders. To family and friends he reveals an affectionate and engaging side of his nature that is easily missed by the casual acquaintance. He likes a good story, and the sharpness of his wit makes for lively conversation. Those who know him well find him a delightful and easy companion.

One is tempted to account for his unusual effectiveness by ascribing to him the possession of ordinary qualities in extraordinary measure, but such an appraisal would leave too much out. He has long been recognized, in the words of another former associate, as "the image of a Christian man and Christian leader." He will be remembered, however, chiefly because he has effected substantial changes in our national life. These contributions to our social history, and to our ecclesiastical pattern, can be explained in part, but only in part, by his unusual ability, energy and devotion to duty. They also rest, as such achievements must always rest, on the foundation of a structure of ideas strong enough to sustain them.

No one would claim for Pidgeon any great eminence as a constructive theologian. The components of his theology were taken from the common stock upon which most of his contemporaries drew. Calvinism contributed its belief in God's active involvement both in individual actions and in public events. His evangelical background impressed on him the importance of personal decision, and it awakened in him a distrust of manipulation from without. This set him against all forms of psychological and social engineering. From the liberalism that permeated even the conservatives of his generation, he took over an optimistic view of human nature based on belief in an innate affinity between God and man.

Some of these ideas, shared by Pidgeon with many of his contemporaries, have for some time been out of fashion among theologians. A revived Calvinism, strongly affected by the existentialism of Kierkegaard, has posited an unbridgeable chasm between man and God; in place of the intimate relation of filial trust that seems to him the natural attitude of the child of God, it has called for a leap of faith into the unknown. He would agree with many contemporary theologians that only a miracle of grace can undo the radical disharmony between fallen man and God. The difference is that miracles, for which disillusioned sceptics of the twentieth century scarcely dare to hope, are for him expected events of daily occurrence, bringing sinners to repentance and transforming the life of the redeemed Christian.

That some of the elements Pidgeon took into his theology were used by many of his contemporaries to construct naïvely optimistic and shallow views of life can scarcely be doubted today. In his hands, however, they provided a blend of ideas unsystematic but consistent, at once workable and thoroughly biblical. He has always maintained a firm grasp on the whole gospel, and doing so he has kept himself free from faddishness or party-line dogmatism. He has held in fine balance Paul's emphasis on faith and John's on love: like Paul he calls for a response to God's action; like John he calls forth our responsiveness to God's being. He sees God's purpose as all of a piece, and therefore he see it as affecting every facet of personal and social life. His thought has a cosmic dimension: all things are summed up in Christ, from which it follows that nothing is too large or too small to be affected by redemption.

If he has a distinctive emphasis of his own, it is upon what he calls the vicarious principle. Not only Christ's death but his whole earthly life and continuing presence are for our sakes, and we are called to respond by showing the same readiness to live in and for others. The Christian ethic is more than a means of working a general improvement in moral standards; it calls for the total investment of the self in God's purpose. This emphasis accords with his whole theology. If each individual is intended to be a complete person, it is so that he may find his rightful place in a universe ordered by a loving God towards the ultimate harmony of all things.

Pidgeon's approach to theology is reminiscent of that of the early Fathers of the Church, who did not delight in paradox but insisted that only the gospel is finally reasonable and pressed home its appeal to "the soul naturally Christian." The early Greek theologians staked a claim for God's sovereignty over the whole of nature both spiritual and material, scandalizing those who stood for spiritual values by insisting on the incarnation of Jesus Christ in the flesh. Later, under the pressure of heresies that were resisted but never quite expelled, the West became tainted with a dualism that exalts spirit above matter and sets divine perfection implacably over against human ineptitude. Pidgeon, growing up with the assumptions of Victorian moralism, did not escape the influence of this dualism. If he had not been so thoroughly imbued with it, indeed, he might have had more sympathy for the revolutionary spirit of the twentieth century. In his preaching, however, he agreed with the Fathers in asserting unequivocally the power of Christ to restore the broken unities in man and nature.

The same emphasis is now being discerned as implicit in the ecumenical movement. What we are witnessing in our time is no mere effort to establish a super-church but a recognition that God's holiness demands our wholeness. Towards this conception Pidgeon gradually felt his way, and in some of his later statements he was ahead of his time. His involvement in social reform, although narrowly moralistic in its original conception, expressed his conviction that every area of life is equally God's. His leadership in the church union movement was rooted in his belief that in Christ we are all bound to each other. His conception of the integrity of God's universe made it impossible for him to divorce spiritual unity from organic union. This same conception of the cosmic completeness of redemption, expressed in more sophisticated terms by some venturesome theologians today, underlay his insistence that "all must come in" at a time when ecumenical discussions were bogged down in the definition of differences. Pidgeon's ecumenical importance has a theological rationale. He has contributed not the daring originality of an inspired prophet but the insight of a saintly student into "the whole counsel of God."